The Beginner's Guide to Flyball

Lisa Pignetti

The Beginner's Guide to Flyball

Cover design: Caroline Woodward

Interior design and layout: Otto Dimitrijevics

Cover photo: Len Silvester

First edition

First printing, 2012

For Vette

(Photo by Willie Moore)

20% of all royalties from this book will go to the National Canine Cancer Foundation in memory of my Border Collie, Vette, and all the other great dogs out there who have battled hemangiosarcoma and other canine cancers.

http://www.wearethecure.org/friends/beginnersguidetoflyball

Table of Contents

Acknowledgments

The idea for this book was born back in in 2007, when I was on the NAFA board of directors. We were tossing around ideas for how to promote and increase public awareness of the sport of flyball and I suggested an "introduction to flyball" type of book. I had no idea that I'd end up writing it, but I'm really glad things worked out the way they did.

This book was self-published, and a ton of people helped me do it. Special thanks to Caroline Woodward, my wonderful friend and visual designer extraordinaire, who not only helped me with all aspects of the design but also kept the book alive in my head with her periodic "How's the book coming along?" emails and phone calls.

Thanks to all the photographers who contributed to this book: Len Silvester, Dave Strauss, Willie Moore, Todd and Stephanie Minnella, Marsha Lundy-Almond, Sam Bennett, and Dave Peake. I spent many happy hours looking through your photo galleries, and got a head rush every time I saw the perfect photo to help illustrate a concept in the book.

Speaking of photos, the cover photo (taken in 2011 at the U-FLI Championship) is one of Len's – it's a picture of Connie Croley's 10-year-old Border Collie Vixen, who was being handled by 13-year-old Riley Erlenbeck on Pawbusters.

Thanks to Dave Thomas for letting me include some of the amazing passing photos captured by his Automated Pass Evaluation System (APES). Advances in technology like this and Andy McBride's FlyballGeek web race application make flyball more fun for everyone.

A lot of people read this book at various stages, and their feedback was enormously helpful: Kyle Mankes, Stephanie Minnella, Leerie Jenkins, Kate Corum, Kristie Austin Pope, Sarah Proctor, and Lisa Gironda.

I also got a lot of ideas and feedback from the gloriously opinionated readers of the Flyball Prop-a-Ganda blog (http://www.flyballpropaganda.

com). Thank you, flyball community – this book was a two-year labor of love, and we all worked on it together.

Thanks to all the people who have taught me so much about flyball over the years, especially Barb Black for introducing Hathaway and me to flyball in the first place. A special shout out to my training buddies and mentors over the years: Jenny Staton, Laura Moretz, Kristie Austin Pope, Stephanie Minnella, Colleen Morita, and the members of Awesome Racing Flyball Fanatics (ARFF), New England Trailblazers, Sirius Competition, Dogsmack, Fetchin' Frenzi, Carpe Pilam, X Flyball, and Lickety Splits, and also to Aaron Robbins and Kelly Robbins-Walt of Rocket Relay who have put on some really kickass seminars (I've been to three! I'm overdue for another one).

Thanks to my partner in life, Todd Murnan, for luring me out to California so we could combine all our dogs and my two kids into one sitcom-worthy household and live happily ever after. To say he's broadened my horizons is an understatement.

Thanks also to my kids, Connor and Greer, for cheerfully sharing their childhood with a pack of dogs, traveling with me to flyball practices and tournaments, and putting up with all this book-writing stuff. A few nights ago, Connor (who's 11) told me that he thought my flyball book was going to help lots of people. (Gahh, no pressure!) I hope he's right.

Introduction

I bet you'll never forget the first time you saw flyball.

Maybe you were flipping through TV channels when Animal Planet was broadcasting a flyball segment. Or you were at an NBA game and flyball was the halftime entertainment. Maybe you watched a flyball demo at the local dog park fundraiser. Or your friend on Facebook, an avid flyball competitor, got your curiosity up with all her flyball-related status updates, photos, and videos.

The first question you probably asked yourself was, "What in the world *is* that?"

The second question was probably, "How can *I* play?!"

I discovered flyball about thirteen years ago when I lived in Massachusetts. My two-year-old Jack Russell Terrier, Hathaway, really needed something to keep him busy, so we spent the cold northeastern winter in beginner's agility class, and in the spring we went to a big agility play-day event with hundreds of other agility wannabes. I looked across the field that day and saw a group of people having flyball practice. I had no idea what they were doing, but Hathaway and I walked over to check it out. The club owner, Barb, explained the game and encouraged me to let Hathaway to investigate the flyball course.

I said, "Hathy, go get that ball" (he was an obsessive fetcher) and he promptly jumped over several of the hurdles, triggered the flyball box and caught the tennis ball, then brought the ball over to me on the sidelines. Barb turned to me and said, "**PLEASE** play flyball with us. We really need a height dog!"

I had no idea what a *height dog* was back then, but apparently it was important.

Since flyball looked really fun and I liked the idea of being on a team, Hathaway and I ditched agility and took up flyball instead.

Fast-forward. Hathaway, now nearly 15, is retired from flyball (but still going strong as of this writing) and I now have a whole pack of dogs, a dizzying array of Border Collies and Border Staffies (Border Collie x Staffordshire Bull Terrier mixes), plus a Belgian Malinois and an Australian Cattle Dog.

Flyball has been a huge influence on my life – it has introduced me to some of my best friends, taken me on adventures all over the U.S. and Canada, and taught me a lot about the wonderful dogs I share my life with. I even met my fiancé, Todd, through my involvement with flyball.

These days I have a blog called *Flyball Prop-a-Ganda* (www.flyball-propaganda.com), where I post articles and carry on discussions about flyball with competitors all over the world. I love talking about flyball and sharing tips and ideas with other flyball enthusiasts. That's what motivated me to write this book.

It has always been hard for newbies to figure out how to get started in flyball. It's sort of a quirky niche dog sport. It doesn't get big media coverage like disc dog or agility. NAFA and U-FLI don't have the budgets or staff for big marketing campaigns, so they rely on flyball competitors to market the sport in a grassroots way. As a result, flyball knowledge and resources are spread across the Internet, and competitors communicate primarily through email lists, Facebook, YouTube, and blogs.

Although flyball has grown every year since its inception in the early eighties, we haven't seen a new flyball book in North America in over 15 years (since Lonnie Olson's *Flyball Racing: The Dog Sport for Everyone* was published in 1997). A lot has changed since then – we've seen the emergence of a new flyball organization (U-FLI), the first sub-15-second world record run, modifications to equipment, multiple rule changes, and radically different training techniques.

The purpose of this book is to give you a crash course in flyball so you can get out there and start competing (and speaking flyball language) as soon as possible. Although flyball is a team sport, there's a lot you can do as an individual to get involved and start training. If you're already training or competing, there are a lot of ideas in here to help you improve. Hopefully this book will save you time and keep you from making some of the same mistakes I did.

Just beware, because before you know it you may find yourself with a house full of dogs, a tricked-out minivan, and a raging flyball addiction.

What is Flyball?

History

Flyball, affectionately called "the rock and roll of dog sports," is a riveting high-speed team sport that attracts tens of thousands of people and their dogs every weekend to tournaments all over North America.

This is Jetson (TCh Emankay Searcher Othnite) on an old flyball box. Jetson belongs to Kerrie Piper and Dave Peake in Victoria, Australia. Kerrie's dad built this box for her when she was young. Kerrie says, "Those were the days when agility was still an add on to the occasional obedience trial and we were looking for something new. We grew up in Nicholson, our local dog club focused on mainly obedience with a touch of agility, and I was too young to drive. So Dad and Mum made up a flyball box and my border collie Jetson and Mum's border collie, GSD and papillon made up the rest of our 'team.'" Jetson was 7 years old in this photo, and is now 14. **(Photo by Dave Peake)**

The whole concept of flyball evolved from scent discrimination hurdle racing back in the 1970s in California. Somebody came up with the idea to add a tennis ball into the game, which led to the creation of a ball-launching device (the first flyball box). In the early 1980s, a dog trainer named Herbert Wagner appeared on *The Tonight Show* with Johnny Carson to demonstrate flyball to the world. The viewing public was so charmed by it that people started forming flyball groups at their local obedience clubs, and the sport took off from there.

Flyball became "official" in 1984, when 12 flyball clubs in Michigan and Ontario formed the North American Flyball Association (NAFA). NAFA was created to standardize the rules, keep records of tournaments, and guide the development of flyball in North America. The first official flyball rulebook was written by Mike Randall, who still plays flyball today with his club Blockade Runners in North Carolina.

In its first 25 years the sport has grown from 12 clubs to over 500 clubs in practically every U.S. state and Canadian province (an average flyball club has about 15-20 members). A second flyball organization called the United Flyball League International (U-FLI) was formed in 2005, and between U-FLI and NAFA there are over 600 tournaments sanctioned in North America every year.

There have been over 100,000 dogs registered with NAFA since 1984 and over 7,500 dogs registered with U-FLI since 2005.

Flyball has grown into a worldwide phenomenon. There are flyball organizations in the United Kingdom, Australia, South Africa, and Japan. Crufts Dog Show in England, the largest annual dog show in the world, now includes a flyball competition as part of their program and broadcasts a video feed online so that people all over the world can watch the racing.

The Game

Flyball in a Nutshell

Flyball is a team relay race competition – four dogs and handlers on one team compete against four dogs and handlers on another team. The teams race each other on a 51-foot course with a start/finish line on one end, a flyball box on the other end, and four hurdles in between.

The object of the game is for all four dogs to run the course without making a mistake, and to do it faster than the opposing team.

The start dogs are released on a set of lights modeled after a drag racing light tree. The dogs race down their lane over the jumps, trigger the box and catch their balls, then turn around and race back to their handlers. The second dogs are then passed into the first dogs (crossing as close to the start/finish line as possible) and they complete the same pattern, until all four dogs have run. If any of the dogs make a mistake – e.g. drop their ball before the finish line, run around a jump, pass the start line before the previous dog passes the finish line, etc. – they have to re-run at the end in order for the team to complete the **heat**. Flyball tournaments consist of multiple races, depending on the number of entries. Each race consists of multiple heats (between 3 and 5).

You can walk into any flyball tournament and the course layout will be the same. This one is in Talladega, Alabama. **(Photo by Sam Bennett)**

Each team's jump height is determined by the **height dog** – the short-est dog on their team.

Each team is allowed to have two alternates, for a total of six dogs in the lineup.

In addition to competing against the team in the opposing lane, there is also the added element of competing against your own personal best time, the personal best times of other clubs, regional time records, and even world records.

Although flyball looks chaotic to the spectator, it is actually quite controlled and carefully choreographed. Each dog and handler knows exactly where to line up, run, and stand/play afterwards. It's sort of like watching an Olympic short-track speed skating relay on TV – it looks a little crazy, but the competitors know what they're doing.

A swirl of activity at the 2011 U-FLI Tournament of Champions, held at the Purina Event Center, just outside of St. Louis, Missouri. **(Photo by Len Silvester)**

Teamwork

Flyball is a team sport, and that makes it different from other dog sports. Most dog sports revolve around relationships between a single handler and a dog, but flyball is built on the notion of clubs and teams. Clubs often become like extended families – you practice together, travel to tournaments together, and celebrate each other's accomplishments in and out of the ring (like birthdays, weddings, and work promotions). You are friends, sometimes the best of friends.

Flyball is competitive, but it's also a family sport – it's common to see spouses competing together and parents in the lane with their kids, teaching them how to race their dogs. You may see a 60-year-old woman and a 12-year-old boy handling dogs on the same team and high-fiving each other after the race. NAFA and U-FLI both have junior handler programs for kids under 18, and their participation and accomplishments are celebrated.

The word **team** is often used interchangeably with **club** (as in "My flyball team rocks!"), but technically you belong to a flyball club, and the flyball club enters a flyball team (or teams) into the tournament. The club I belong to has about ten members and usually enters two or three teams into each tournament. Our teams vary from tournament to tournament, depending on who can travel and which dogs are available.

NAFA and U-FLI also allow people from different clubs to form teams and run their dogs together during a tournament – this option is called "Open class" in NAFA and a "Pickup team" in U-FLI. It's great for people who are traveling to another region without their club, or who want to race with their friends from another club just for fun one weekend.

There is a team within a team, too – you and your dog. Flyball forms a strong bond between you and your dog because you spend a lot of time training together, traveling together, and competing together. Flyball is fun, exciting, and full of rewards, and your dog will come to associate you with all these things. Flyball is also a great outlet for your dog's natural energy and prey drive.

Flyball can be a significant time commitment – you can spend a lot of time training (some dogs learn quickly but others may take over a year before they're ready to compete), and tournaments will take up your entire weekend, plus the travel time on either end. Your club will be relying on you, too – if you commit to going to a tournament, you can't change your mind at the last minute or you'll be leaving everybody in a lurch.

Tournament formats

At each tournament, teams are sorted into divisions based on the type of team they are and how fast they are (teams send in a **seed time** with their entry, which is an estimate of how fast they think that team will run at the tournament). Organizing teams by seed times ensures competitive divisions and tight races no matter how fast the teams are. Most tournaments offer the following classes:

- **Regular:** any four dogs from the same club.

- **Multibreed** (NAFA) or **Variety** (U-FLI): four different breeds from the same club – mixes count as only one "breed." For example, you might see a Border Collie, a Golden Retriever, a mixed-breed dog, and a Jack Russell Terrier together.

- **Open** (NAFA) or **Pickup** (U-FLI): any four dogs from any club.

- **Veterans** (NAFA only): any four dogs from any club seven years old or over.

- **Singles** racing and **Pairs** racing (U-FLI only): one dog (singles) or a pair of dogs (pairs), from any club.

Tournament directors have several different racing formats to choose from, so you'll see variations from region to region. Sometimes teams race in a round robin format, other times they'll compete in an elimination tournament, sometimes it's a combination of both (like round robin on the first day to determine seeding for an elimination tournament the second day).

Tournaments usually take place on a Saturday and Sunday, although you'll see the occasional one that starts on Friday night.

Club tournament options include:

Two one-day tournaments:

- Separate results and awards each day

- Teams can change their rosters and lineups each day

- Generally a higher entry fee across both days (since the host club is paying extra in tournament fees to NAFA or U-FLI, plus buying two sets of awards)

One two-day tournament:

- Points accumulate over both days

- Rosters and lineups must remain the same over the course of the weekend

- One set of awards is given at the end of the tournament, based on two days' worth of results

- More common in NAFA than U-FLI

Cost

As far as dog sports go, flyball is a pretty good bargain. A single team entry fee for an entire weekend of racing is usually around $150 – split four ways (or more, if you have five or six dogs on the team and are rotating dogs in), you're looking at about $35-40 per dog. Tournament directors usually try to get each team 30-40 heats of racing (which translates into 6-8 races) over the weekend, so you and your dog will probably be running a lot, too.

Add to that the cost of a hotel room (often shared with team members), gas, and food, plus whatever rewards you're bringing for your dog (treats, tugs, floppy discs, etc.), and that's about all you'll need to pay for a weekend of flyball.

Flyball equipment can be pricey, but the big ticket items like flyball boxes ($500-$1,300) are a one-time investment and are usually paid for at the club level, not by individuals. The same goes for floor matting (most tournaments are run on anti-fatigue floor mats to prevent injuries to the dogs' paws) – you won't need matting unless you're practicing regularly on concrete or hosting tournaments, and the cost usually gets spread across the club. Jumps can easily be made out of plywood, and props can be made from inexpensive items found in Lowe's or Home Depot like white plastic PVC pipe and plastic rain gutters.

If you want to get started at home, you can make a ramp out of plywood to train your dog the basics of getting on and off the flyball box. You can pick up some used tennis balls at a tennis club (they will often give them to you for free, by the bag full) or at a used sporting equipment store like Play It Again Sports. You can make a set of wooden jumps out of a 4-foot by 8-foot sheet of plywood then spray them with a can of white spray paint (a quick Google search will yield plenty of examples). These jumps can double as props (training aids). Voila – you are ready to start training, for less than $50.

Organizations

There are currently two flyball sanctioning bodies in North America – NAFA and U-FLI. NAFA is a non-profit organization run by elected volunteers and U-FLI is a for-profit corporation comprised of owners and shareholders.

U-FLI was established in 2005 by a group of competitors who wanted an alternative to NAFA. The presence of both organizations has been very positive for the growth of flyball.

Although both flavors of flyball are played all over North America, you'll generally see NAFA played in Canada and the eastern half of the U.S. and U-FLI played in the western half of the U.S.

The two organizations' rules are very similar, the key differences being how height dogs are measured and the types of racing divisions offered.

Lots of competitors play both NAFA and U-FLI, just like a lot of agility folks play both USDAA and AKC agility. Most competitors don't really care which organization they're supporting, they just want to play flyball as often (and as close to home) as possible. Aside from the one-time cost to register your dog with each organization ($25 or less), there's not much you need to do differently from one organization to another.

Titles and Awards

Points and titles are an important part of flyball. Dogs earn points when their team completes clean heats under a certain time period, and the points accumulate over time into titles. Both NAFA and U-FLI maintain public databases (accessible from their websites) where competitors can track points and titles obtained for any dog that competes.

🐕 *Rukus is an 11-year-old Mini Aussie owned by Gord and Elva Bradley of Ontario. On Sept 15, 2012, Rufus became the top-pointed dog in the history of NAFA with 154,909 points (this photo is from that actual tournament). He races with the DOG-ON-IT flyball team.* **(Photo by Marsha Lundy-Almond)**

Points requirements for NAFA:

- Under 24 seconds: each dog earns 25 points per heat.

- 24 to 27.999 seconds: each dog earns 5 points per heat.

- 28 to 31.999 seconds: each dog earns 1 point per heat.

NAFA's titles:

Title	Points
Flyball Dog (FD)	20
Flyball Dog Excellent (FDX)	100
Flyball Dog Champion (FDCh)	500
Flyball Dog Champion – Silver (FDCh-S)	1,000
Flyball Dog Champion – Gold (FDCh-G)	2,500
Flyball Master (FM)	5,000

Title	Points
Flyball Master Excellent (FMX)	10,000
Flyball Master Champion (FMCh)	15,000
Onyx	20,000
Flyball Grand Champion (FGDCh)	30,000
(no title, but commemorative pin and plaque for each of these milestones)	40,000 – 90,000 (at 10,000 point increments)
Hobbes Award	100,0000
Iron Dog Award	Awarded to dogs who earn at least one point a year for 10 consecutive years.

This is Hobbes, the Collie/Shepherd mix owned by Gary & Julie Mueller. Hobbes became the first NAFA dog ever to reach 100,000 points, and the Hobbes Award was created and named after him in 2006. He was also inducted into the Clyde Moore Memorial Hall of Fame in 2004. Hobbes retired from the Ballistics team in 2004, with 109,301 points. He passed away at age 16 in 2008. **(Photo by Len Silvester)**

At this writing, 30 dogs have earned over 100,000 points in NAFA, making them part of the esteemed "Hobbes Award" club (named after Hobbes, a Collie/Shepherd mix in Canada who was the first dog ever to reach 100,000 points in 2002).

Points requirements for U-FLI:

- Under 20 seconds: each dog earns 30 points per heat.

- 20 to 24.999: each dog earns 25 points per heat.

- 25 to 29.999: each dog earns 15 points per heat.

- 30 to 35.000: each dog earns 10 points per heat.

U-FLI also awards 5 bonus points per heat to the dogs on the winning team of that heat.

U-FLI's Award Pins:

Title	Points
Top Flight (TF)	100
TF-I	500
TF-II	750
TF-III	1,000
Top Flight Executive (TFE)	2,500
TFE-I	4,000
TFE-II	5,500
TFE-III	7,000
Top Flight Premier (TFP)	9,500
TFP-I	12,000
TFP-II	14,500
TFP-III	17,500

Title	Points
Top Flight First Class	20,500
TFFC-I	24,000
TFFC-II	27,500
TFFC-III	31,000
Top Flight World Class (TFWC)	35,500
TFWC-I	40,000
TFWC-II	44,500
TFWC-III	49,000
Top Flight X-treme (TFX)	54,500
TFX-I	60,000
TFX-II	65,500
TFX-III	71,000
Top Flight Ultimate (TFU)	77,500
TFU-I	84,000
TFU-II	90,500
TFU-III	97,000

U-FLI Milestone Plaques:

Title	Points
Top Flight Expert	20,000
Top Flight Ace	35,000
Top Flight Champion	50,000
Top Flight Specialist	75,000
Top Flight Elite	100,000

I'm personally not a big points tracker. We all play flyball for different reasons, and I get more enjoyment out of racing as fast as possible, which usually means my team is earning less points due to early passes and unfinished heats. I do love seeing green dogs earn their first titles, and I'm always happy about my dogs' big milestone titles (like NAFA's 20,000-point Onyx award, for instance), but otherwise I don't usually know how many points my dogs have.

Some competitors (and some entire clubs) are avid points/title accumulators, and they create team lineups based on what will earn the most points for each dog in the club. This means they may split up their fastest dogs across teams so that each team's average time per heat will fall under 20 seconds (U-FLI) or 24 seconds (NAFA), earning the four running dogs on the team maximum points.

Some clubs really go all out with their points celebrations, creating quilts, framed photos, and other keepsakes to document milestone titles. It's nice to celebrate accomplishments, whatever your goals may be. And it's great when you play flyball in a club where you all agree on what is important and you work together to make that happen. Teamwork is what flyball is all about.

In addition to points and titles, NAFA also has three annual awards:

- **Clyde Moore Memorial Hall of Fame:** Dogs can be nominated by any individual, then the list is pared down by the NAFA board of directors and voted on by the **delegates** (NAFA clubs who have earned votes through their tournament participation). One or two new dogs are inducted into the NAFA Hall of Fame each year.

- **Regional Most Valuable Player (MVP):** Dogs can be nominated for Regional MVP by any club in their region and are voted on by the NAFA delegates in that region each year.

- **Judge of the Year:** Eligible judges (those who are currently a NAFA judge and have been one for at least five years) can be nominated by any individual, then the list is pared down by the NAFA board of directors and voted on by the delegates.

🐕 *This is the legendary Radar, a big red tri-colored Border Collie owned by Aaron Robbins of Rocket Relay in Hamilton, Ontario. Radar was one of the fastest dogs of his time and helped Rocket Relay set many world records. Radar passed away in 2009 at the age of 14. He was inducted into the Clyde Moore Memorial Hall of Fame later that year.* **(Photo by Len Silvester)**

NAFA and U-FLI also host large national championship tournaments every year. For a while NAFA's championship was part of the United States Dog Agility Association's (USDAA) World Cynosport Games, but in recent years it has become a standalone event called the NAFA CanAm Classic. The tournament is open to any NAFA club and offers unlimited Regular, Multibreed, Open, and Veterans classes of racing. There are also two special tournament-specific classes – CanAm Regular and CanAm Multibreed. The CanAm classes race on Sunday and are by invitation only (based on the fastest times from the Regular and Multibreed racing on Saturday). The CanAm Classic is a HUGE tournament, with racing going on in six rings at the same time.

U-FLI's Tournament of Champions is open to clubs who qualify during the year at one of the U-FLI qualification tournaments held throughout the U.S. and Canada (there are usually six or seven to pick from).

🐕 *View from behind the boxloaders at the 2012 NAFA CanAm Classic.*
(Photo by Dave Strauss)

Clubs qualify by division based on their fastest time at a U-FLI tournament during the year, and can become the champion of their division. U-FLI currently recognizes champions in nine different divisions, which range based on seed times (for example, Division 1 is for teams that run 15.699 seconds or faster, Division 2 is 15.700-16.099 seconds, Division 3 is 16.100-16.499 seconds, and so on.)

World Records

As of this writing, the NAFA world record (Regular division) is held by Rocket Relay of Hamilton, Canada. On September 2nd, 2012, they ran 14.931 seconds with two Border Collies, a Belgian Malinois, and a mixed-breed height dog over 8-inch jumps.

Spring Loaded of Michigan holds the NAFA Multibreed record. On September 5, 2004, they ran 15.36 seconds with a Border Collie, a Dutch Shepherd, a mixed-breed dog, and a Whippet.

The U-FLI world record is currently held by Touch N Go of Las Vegas, NV. In 2009, they were the first flyball team to ever break the 15-second barrier, and on December 2, 2011, they ran 14.690 with four mixed-breed dogs (two Border Staffies and two Border Whippets). U-FLI only recognizes records for the Regular division, not Variety (aka Multibreed).

A buoyant Rocket Relay in September 2012, just after breaking the NAFA world record (Regular division), and becoming the first NAFA team to ever break the 15-second barrier (with a 14.931). **(Photo by Saywoof.ca)**

The Flyball Dog

What Makes a Good Flyball Dog

One great thing about flyball is that all types of dogs – purebreds and mixed breeds, big dogs and little dogs – are welcome to play and have something valuable to offer a team.

Sure, the fastest teams are usually dominated by Border Collies and Border Collie mixes (designer mixes bred on purpose for flyball), but if you go to a tournament you will see all kinds of dogs racing in the various divisions, earning points and titles and having a blast. The more unusual breeds are actually the most fun to watch – the giant Great Dane loping over the hurdles, the tiny determined Dachshund leaping up onto the box to get the ball, the flashy Shar Pei with the gorgeous swimmer's turn. Flyball would be boring if it were just a bunch of Border Collies running around.

*Teddy is a two-year-old mini Labradoodle owned by Mandy Kincer. Teddy, who is very ball motivated and runs in the low 4's, runs with Reeking Havoc Flyball Team of Southern Ohio. **(Photo by Len Silvester)***

Being consistent and reliable has great value, just like being a speed demon has great value. Even the smallest dogs have an important role in flyball – they are the coveted height dogs.

I'll delve into more of what makes a good flyball dog later in the book, but the two most important attributes are:

- The dog must be physically sound (able to run and jump without stress or pain).

- The dog must be able to get along with (or at least ignore) other dogs and humans in a loud, chaotic environment.

Almost everything else can be trained.

Dogs LOVE flyball – you'll notice this when you're watching them at flyball practice, or at a demo, or during a tournament. Many of them claw to get out of their crates, drag their handlers across the tournament site, and lunge and bark like crazy dogs as they wait to get into the lane.

This dog is ready to go! Capone is a blue merle Border Collie owned by Nora Rowland of Wisconsin. Even though he has very crazy eyes in this photo, outside of flyball he's a therapy dog who works in hospitals. The red merle looking on eagerly is Tundra, owned by Cheryl Lewis. **(Photo by Len Silvester)**

Flyball taps into a dog's natural prey drive – they get to race another dog down to the box as fast as they can to catch a tennis ball, then run back as fast as they can to catch their handler (who is usually teasing them by running in the opposite direction) and grab a tug toy, which seems to come alive when their handler is tugging with them.

What's a "fast" dog in flyball?

Most dogs run the flyball course in between 4.0 and 7.0 seconds. A dog is considered to be particularly fast if it consistently runs under 4.0 seconds – "sub-4" is the common term you'll hear for that. The majority of sub-4 dogs run in the 3.8 or 3.9 range, with a few elite dogs clocking in at 3.5, 3.6, or 3.7. The fastest time I've ever heard of is 3.4, run by several different Whippets and Border Collie x Whippet mixes in 2011 and 2012.

A fast height dog (especially in NAFA, where height dogs jump proportionately higher than in U-FLI) would be a dog that consistently runs in the low 4's (4.0-4.3 range). A sub-4 second height dog is truly gold.

The amazing Dragon, owned by Stephanie Minnella. Dragon (Poeta Clambake Carnival) is a three-year-old Whippet and runs on X Flyball in Southern California. His best time to date is 3.48. **(Photo by Todd V. Minnella)**

No matter how fast your dog is, as he gains experience and gets into his groove (with striding and his box turn), his times will continue to drop until they reach the point where they level out and become remarkably consistent. I can predict what my dogs will run down to the tenth of a second most of the time. For example, I have one Border Collie who, if she runs in start position, will run 4.0 in almost every single heat all weekend (slowing down to 4.1 late Sunday afternoon).

Every tenth of a second improvement that you make in your dog's average time (with more training, conditioning, etc.) is a major accomplishment.

Height Dogs

The **height dog** is the canine team member who sets the jump height for the other three dogs on his team.

To determine a dog's jump height in NAFA, a judge uses a wicket to measure the dog in inches from the ground to their withers (the area on their back near their shoulder blades). They round any fractions down to the nearest inch, then subtract 5 inches from that measurement to get the jump height.

*Lucky is a Cairn Terrier owned by Debbie Harrie in California. He runs with Woof Gang over his U-FLI jump height of 6 inches. **(Photo by Len Silvester)***

For example, if you have a Jack Russell Terrier who measures 14½ inches at the withers, you would first round the measurement down to 14 inches, then subtract five more inches to get a jump height of 9 inches.

NAFA requires dogs to race for one full year before they can apply for a height card. The height card is optional. Having it in your wallet means you won't have to wake up quite so early on the Saturday morning of a tournament to get your dog measured, although these days most competitors don't bother getting a height card. In fact, many people don't even bother having their dog measured after they've had it officially measured by a judge a few times (so that they and the other competitors in their region know what its jump height is). They start just showing up to race on Saturday mornings and setting up their hurdles at that jump height. Other teams can challenge a dog's height (as long as they're racing in the same division) and the head judge can measure a dog's height anytime at his discretion, but these things rarely happen.

Simon is a four-year-old Toy Fox Terrier owned by Susan Floer. He runs with Reeking Havoc Flyball Team of Southern Ohio. Simon weighs 7 pounds and stands about 10 inches tall, and runs in the mid 5-second range. He holds the breed record in U-FLI for Toy Fox Terriers. A little dog and a big asset! **(Photo by Len Silvester)**

To determine a dog's jump height in U-FLI, a judge uses a special caliper device to measure the length of the dog's leg from the point of their elbow to their accessory carpal bone (the bony protrusion just above the carpal pad), then assigns the dog a lifetime jump height based on this number. Dogs can be officially measured once they are over a year old, and that one measurement is good for the rest of its U-FLI racing career.

NAFA's jump heights range from a minimum of 7 inches to a maximum of 14 inches. U-FLI's range is smaller with a minimum of 6 inches to a maximum of 12 inches.

Dogs are generally considered to be height dogs if they measure for a jump height of 11 inches or less – that's the magic cut-off number for some reason. With proper conditioning, most dogs (who measure for 11 inch jump heights or are taller than that) race just fine over 11 inches. In fact, the previous NAFA Regular world record holders, Spring Loaded, achieved their world record with an 11-inch jump height. But once dogs are jumping 12 inches or more, their speed and performance take a big hit.

Dogs that would never be used as height dogs in NAFA (because they would jump 12 inches or over) can easily measure for a 9- or 10-inch jump height in U-FLI.

There are a few classes of racing where you won't need to worry about height dogs: NAFA's Veterans class, where all the dogs are 7 years old or over (so they jump the minimum jump height for safety reasons), and U-FLI's singles and pairs racing, where you get to choose your own jump height (6 inch minimum).

Evaluating Your Dog

There have been times when people brought dogs to flyball class or practice that I secretly thought would never play flyball, and I turned out to be wrong. Sometimes dogs that initially seem to have no drive, or love to chase other dogs, or have zero interest in tennis balls "turn on" with the right training and become great flyball dogs. (And, on the flip side of that, not all Border Collies or Jack Russell Terriers are flyball superstars.)

As I mentioned before, there are a few critical requirements when it comes to playing flyball:

- Your dog should be fit and healthy.
- Your dog should not be aggressive towards other dogs or people.

Fitness

Your dog may run the flyball course 40-60 times over a weekend, counting the total number of heats plus re-runs, false starts, and warm-ups. So it's really important that he get plenty of exercise to build up his endurance and pack as little extra weight as possible.

Extra weight on your dog can increase his risk of injury (especially over time from repetitive strain) and cause him to tucker out partway through a tournament.

Don't rely on the dog food bag to tell you how much you should be feeding your dog. Most feeding guides on dog food bags show you a sliding scale based on weight – according to them, the more your dog weighs, the more he needs to eat. That's ridiculous! It's like telling a 400-pound person that they should be eating more than the average person because they weigh more.

To keep my dogs flyball fit, I feed them a good quality high protein kibble twice a day and keep them borderline "skinny." If you run your hands lightly over their sides, you will feel a little bit of their ribs. My vet is really supportive of this and often comments during exams about how low their resting heart rate is and how healthy their organs are.

One safe, easy way to take a few pounds off your dog is to replace half their kibble with canned green beans (sodium free) for a couple of weeks. I also mix in a tablespoon or two of canned pumpkin (plain, without added spices) as a binder – dogs LOVE green beans and pumpkin. It fills them up but has a lot less fat/calories.

Consult with your vet if you have specific questions about diet and exercise – make sure you explain to them that you have an *athlete*, not a normal house dog.

There are tons of great ways to condition your dogs, and the more variety they get the better. You can take them to a pool or lake to swim, run them hard while playing a fun game like Frisbee or fetch (a Chuckit, a pile of tennis balls, and a big field is a really easy way to tire out a bunch of dogs fast), put them on a treadmill (yes, really!), and take them on hikes through the woods or runs through the neighborhood. Wrestling with other dogs and playing tug with you also counts as exercise. At flyball practice you can do power-jumping drills, where you put six or seven jumps in a row (10 feet apart) and do recalls for 5-10 minutes at a time to build up their endurance.

Sage, Dragon, Maverick and Seek of X Flyball getting a great workout while having fun. **(Photo by Stephanie Minnella)**

Flyball is a short sprint, but it's a lot of short sprints in a row. Your dog will need sprint conditioning as well as distance conditioning. Chuckit and Frisbee (especially on a hill) are great for this.

The time you put into your dog's conditioning and fitness will pay off in the flyball lanes. I've known dogs' times to improve several tenths of a second (which is a lot, in flyball-land) once they dropped a few pounds and were exercised more.

Aggression

There's no place for aggression in flyball competition. Your dog will be constantly surrounded by a sea of other dogs at practice and tournaments. The environment is highly charged – many dogs bark and pull on their leashes to get into the racing lanes, and space can be tight sometimes next to the ring. Part of the game is that your dog will have to pass within inches of another dog at the start/finish line (at top speed), then come back to you in a **runback area** (the place where all the handlers and dogs line up to race and run back to afterwards) full of other barking and tugging dogs. For the majority of the race, you will not have your hands or a leash on your dog, so he is free to make his own decisions.

Your dog doesn't have to *like* other dogs or people, but he does have to be able to tolerate them or ignore them.

A couple of my dogs can be snarky if another dog gets right in their face, but being a little snarky if somebody invades your personal space is very different from straight-up aggression, where you worry that your dog could attack another dog or person with the intent to hurt them.

Your dog needs to be 100% focused on his job, preferably to the point that he doesn't even notice the dog he's passing into or anybody in the runback area. (If your dog isn't at this point yet, don't stress – you can desensitize him to a lot of outside stimuli during training – but it's important that he is not prone to unprovoked aggression.)

Both flyball organizations have strict penalties for aggression. Judges will disqualify and write up dogs that attack other dogs (or even dogs that chase other dogs, if it's clear that the intent is to hurt the other dog), and your dog will only get a few warnings before he's banned from racing permanently.

If you aren't sure if your dog is flyball material, enlist the advice and help of a local behaviorist or trainer.

Finding Flyball in Your Area

Finding a Club or Class

There are hundreds of flyball clubs all over North America, so chances are there's at least one near you.

If you find a flyball club in your area, don't be shy about reaching out to them. They usually have their contact information posted prominently on their website, and most clubs are on a never-ending quest for new teammates. If they're not recruiting, they can probably point you to another club nearby who is.

Some clubs offer formal classes in addition to their practices. They'll usually charge for classes, but the good part is that you'll get their undivided attention for an hour or so, whereas at practice they'll just work you in where they can.

Here are some places to look for clubs and classes:

Club Locators

NAFA and U-FLI both have club locators on their websites, so that's the first place I would go:

- NAFA's Flyball Locator: http://www.flyball.org/getstarted
- U-FLI's Club Locator: http://www.u-fli.com/clublocator.php

There are also a number of flyball-related Yahoo groups (http://groups.yahoo.com) you can join. They are usually organized regionally (U-FLI doesn't recognize regions, but NAFA does). Find out which NAFA region you're in, because it will help you decide which groups to join and which tournaments you'll be attending. The NAFA locator mentioned above has links to all the regional Yahoo groups, plus the name of the regional director (RD) for each region. The RD is NAFA's representative for that region and it's their job to help you out, so email them and ask them to put you in touch with local clubs.

Also, flyball competitors love to talk and share information about the sport, so don't be shy about approaching the competitors (just make sure you catch them when they're not getting ready to go into the ring to race).

The Web

Google the word "flyball" plus the name of your area. It's a quick way to see if any local clubs' websites come up – this is how a lot of people seem to find me. I've gotten more email queries due to random Google searches than either of the organizations' club locators.

Local Obedience or Kennel Clubs

Sometimes you'll find flyball classes taught at a local obedience club, kennel club, or even an AKC breed club. Although their public classes usually tend more towards obedience or conformation handling, it's possible that they have a flyball enthusiast on board who has talked them into supporting a flyball class. Call or email around. Even if they don't have classes planned, they may have a member or two that plays flyball.

Tournaments

Another way to find clubs is to travel to a tournament in your area. You can find tournament listings on the NAFA and U-FLI websites:

- NAFA: http://www.flyball.org/tournaments.html
- UFLI: http://www.u-fli.com/tournreport.php

You might as well get used to driving to tournaments, because that's going to be your life if you join a club and become addicted to flyball. Most of the regional tournaments I attend are at least 2 ½ hours away from me, sometimes much farther than that. It's all part of the adventure. I've been all over the place to play flyball – at least 14 different U.S. states, plus Ontario, Canada.

Once you get to a tournament, make your way inside to the racing (it's always free for spectators) and ask somebody who looks like they know what they're doing to point out the regional director (if you're at a NAFA tournament) or the U-FLI representative (if you're at a U-FLI tournament). RD's and U-FLI reps are great about taking newbies under their wing – they can answer your questions and introduce you to local club owners right there at the tournament.

Dog-related events

Lots of flyball demos take place at dog-related events that benefit local humane societies, dog parks, vet clinics, or pet stores.

Keep your eyes open for news or flyers about these kinds of events and research to see if a flyball demo is included. It's a great way to make contact with a local flyball enthusiast who has some equipment and training.

Craigslist

Believe it or not, I have run across several flyball-related listings on Craigslist (http://www.craigslist.org) recently. People are recruiting new members for their flyball clubs, asking for volunteers to help line judge at their tournaments, advertising their flyball classes, or looking for other people to practice with. You could even post a flyball-wanted ad on Craigslist yourself. It's free.

Don't get discouraged if you can't find a club near you. People are always moving around and forming new clubs, so something may pop up. You can also start your own club.

Starting Your Own Club

People start their own clubs for all sorts of reasons. The obvious one is what we've just been talking about – there are no clubs in your area and you really want to get involved with the sport, so it makes sense to start your own club and become "official."

Philosophies

People often start out in a flyball club together because of simple geographic proximity – it makes sense to want to practice as close to home as possible.

It's important, however, to find (or start) a club with people that you like and with whom you feel comfortable. A lot of flyball clubs become like a big family. You argue and complain like a family, too, but it's okay (when you're with the right people). It's nice to find friends who share your crazy love for dogs. You can help each other train, offer advice and encouragement, help each other meet goals, and get each other through tough times.

So, when you start or join a club, make sure you know what you're getting into up front. Clubs come in all shapes and sizes – some are more competitive, some are more laid back, some practice twice a week, some practice once a month, some require you to pay club dues, some don't.

Club structure

Here are some questions to ask if you're starting your own club:

- How often do you want to practice?

- Are you going to require members to pay dues?

- Who will pay for the equipment? (and what happens to the equipment if your club splits up or individuals leave?)

- Who will store the equipment and bring it to practices and tournaments?

- Are you going to run the club like a democracy or a dictatorship?

- Do you plan to teach classes?

- What's your club name going to be?

- What's your club logo going to look like?

- What color/type of uniform or t-shirt are you all going to wear (and who are you going to order them from)?

- Who's going to create and maintain your club's website?

Some clubs get very formal, drafting bylaws and electing a president, vice president, and treasurer. Some set up their clubs like a non-profit organization. Others are offshoots of obedience clubs, agility clubs, AKC breed clubs, or kennel clubs, and operate under the rules of the parent organization. Most are just groups of people casually banded together under the club name.

Of all the clubs I've been in (seven or eight total), the best ones have been run by experienced, fair leaders who called the shots and made all the final decisions but solicited input from club members along the way.

The **club owner** is the person who officially establishes the club with NAFA and/or U-FLI. They're the only person from the club with whom NAFA or U-FLI is going to communicate. Sometimes club duties are divided up so that an organized financially-savvy person in the club is in charge of the money and of making sure all the paperwork gets filled out and taken care of (e.g., tournament entries, tournament fees) and another person with great training and handling skills is in charge of the actual teams themselves (e.g., training, creating lineups, working with new dogs during warm-ups).

Most clubs set up a bank account in the club's name. Some don't charge any dues at all, they just expect people to pay for their dog's tournament fees and to split the cost of any equipment. Other clubs ask members to pay a monthly or yearly fee, and then use the money they have in the bank to pre-pay tournament fees (with the expectation that members will pay the club back), and also to pay for equipment, building rental, or whatever else your club needs.

If your club is planning to host a tournament and expects to make money off of it, you'll need to decide beforehand what you want to do with that money. Most clubs put it into the club bank account and regularly keep the other club members in the know about the balance and any money that is spent: your club's rules can be as formal as you want them to be.

When I formed my own club I ran it more like a democracy (granting myself and a couple of other close teammates veto power). We didn't charge dues, but because we put on a few profitable tournaments we set up a club bank account and put everything we earned from tournaments in there. We used that money to pay our tournament fees in advance, then asked people to pay the bank account back as soon as they could (and we nagged them until they did it). When we needed new flyball boxes, we used the money in the club bank account to buy them. It was pretty simple, but we also trusted each other. You'll just have to use your own judgment when it comes to managing your club.

I loved being a club owner (I had great teammates, which really helped) but it was also a lot of pressure – coming up with lineups that everybody was happy with, making sure tournament entries made it in on time, getting commitments from people, getting money from people, organizing practices, helping newbies with their dogs, and fielding phone calls and emails from prospects. And there's always at least one argumentative personality in the bunch, who asks why their dog isn't on the competitive "A" team or doesn't get as many points as they want him to.

A good leader takes into consideration all the dogs and their quirks and their owners' goals, and puts together lineups where everybody can pass well, earn lots of points, and run at their fastest potential.

Making It Official

Creating a new club with NAFA or U-FLI is actually quite simple and inexpensive ($25 for NAFA and $20 for U-FLI).

Coming up with a name you like that isn't already taken is the hard part (it's sort of like trying to find a unique domain name on the Web these days!). You can scroll through the registered club names on the NAFA and U-FLI websites for inspiration. Some of them are really clever or funny. NAFA has over 950 registered clubs and U-FLI has nearly 400.

Here's how to register a new club with NAFA:

- Go to the NAFA website: http://www.flyball.org

- On the NAFA home page, you'll see a drop-down menu with a list of forms in it (called "Quick jump to NAFA forms"). Choose the "New Club Registration" form – C.11. (This form is also in the appendix of the NAFA rulebook.)

- Fill out the one-page C.11 form, naming yourself as the club owner.

- You don't have to worry about the CRN# section at the bottom of the form (a CRN is the Competition Racing Number assigned to each dog). When a dog runs in a tournament with your club, his name will automatically be added onto your club's dog listing as part of NAFA's points tracking system.

- Mail the completed form plus a check for $25 to NAFA and you're all set. NAFA will contact you via U.S. Mail (and possibly email, these days) within a few weeks to let you know what your club number is (you'll need this club number to enter tournaments).

- You can get your club's stats and information at the NAFA database: http://nafadb.flyball.org/public.shtml

Here's how to register a new club with U-FLI:

- Go to the U-FLI website: http://www.u-fli.com

- You'll need to have your own participant number before you register a club, so do that first. On the U-FLI home page, choose "Register" then "New Participant" from the top navigation bar.

- Fill out the online form. You can leave the club affiliation set to "No Club Affiliation" at this point.

- Write down your participant number and password, because you'll need them to register your club.

- Then, in the top navigation bar, choose "Register" then "New Club."

- Fill out the form with the required info and submit it. U-FLI charges $20 to register your club. You should get a confirmation email back from U-FLI with your club's number in it.

Attracting Members

If you start advertising your club all over town, pretty soon people are going to be coming out of the woodwork to practice with you.

Create a simple website with your desired practice location/days/times and your contact information clearly visible so people can find you via search engines like Google.

Also design a flyer and put it up anywhere you think dog owners will see it – veterinarians' offices, pet shops, dog day cares, kennel clubs, wherever obedience or agility classes are held, dog parks, and boarding kennels.

Once your club has some equipment and a few dogs completing full runs of the flyball course, volunteer to put on flyball demos at local dog events to drum up even more interest.

Flyball Equipment

One thing I really like about flyball is that the course is the same no matter where you compete. The running surface itself varies – the ring can be set up on grass, concrete with mats, or even hard-packed dirt – but the actual measurements of the course are exactly the same. Prior to every tournament a judge confirms that everything meets the specs in the rulebook.

View from behind the handlers, taken right as the race is about to begin.
(Photo by Len Silvester)

Flyball gets dissed sometimes (by people who compete in other dogs sports, like agility) for being so predictable, but I have never found this predictability boring. On the contrary – I feel like I can really finesse my training, set goals, and see progress because the parameters are always the same. If my dog gets his best time at a tournament, I know it's really his best time ever, because the course measurements were exactly the same, and sophisticated electronic equipment captured his time down to the thousandth of a second.

Flyball also never gets boring thanks to the team aspect of the sport. My club changes its lineups at practically every tournament based on who's available that weekend (plus, green dogs are always moving out of warm-up slots and into the lineup). So at every tournament there's this nervous excitement to see how the four dogs on each of our teams will click together, plus I usually have a new pass to learn. I also love working with the green dogs in warm-ups and seeing their progress.

No matter where you compete – whether it's three hours from home or on the other side of the country – when you walk into the ring to race it'll feel like home to you.

For both NAFA and U-FLI, the course is nearly identical:

- Each lane is 51 feet long from the start/finish line to the flyball box.

- The start/finish line is 6 feet away from the first jump.

- Each jump is 10 feet apart.

- The last jump is 15 feet away from the front of the flyball box.

- The lanes can be no closer than 8 feet apart (NAFA) or 10 feet apart (U-FLI), and no farther than 17 feet apart (NAFA) or 20 feet apart (U-FLI).

- NAFA's minimum runback is 50 feet and U-FLI's is 44 feet.

Balls

Balls are a pretty important piece of equipment – the game is called fly-BALL, after all.

Your choices extend far past the regular yellow-green fuzzy tennis ball. The rules state that the ball must behave like a tennis ball, meaning it should roll, bounce, and shoot out of the box appropriately. So a racquet-ball is okay, but a rock is not. In recent years, relaxable foam balls have become very popular because they are easier for the dog to catch and hold.

They're also great to use if you have a ball-obsessed dog (yes, you can have too much of a good thing) because some dogs don't like the foam balls as much as regular tennis balls. The foam balls come in several different sizes and usually look like they belong at a kid's birthday party, often designed to look like a smiley face or baseball. You can find them at places like Oriental Trading Company and Party City.

A cheerful foam ball mixed in with the regular tennis balls. **(Photo by Dave Strauss)**

If you have a terrier, be careful letting them play with the foam balls longer than five seconds, because they love to kill them (and the balls are a little pricey, around a dollar each).

There are also some variations on the tennis ball that people like to use. Smaller dogs do great with miniature tennis balls (1 ½-inch or 2-inch size) because they fit better in their mouths. And those low compression tennis balls (the ones marketed to kids taking beginner tennis lessons) are easier for some dogs to catch, too.

Steer clear of noise-making balls, like balls that squeak or have bells in them. They aren't permitted at tournaments because they can distract dogs on the other team.

🐕 *This is Katie, a Miniature Long Hair Dachshund owned by Maxine Ray in North Carolina. Katie, who is on Max Fast Flyball team, is quite fond of mini pink leopard print balls.*

You'll need to experiment until you find what's right for your dog.

Sometimes the miniature tennis balls shoot out of the flyball box unpredictably because the hole is cut for a regular size 2 ½-inch tennis ball, so watch to see which type of ball your dog is catching the best.

I really try hard to train all my dogs to catch a plain old tennis ball – it really makes life easier. But it's nice knowing you have options.

Flyball Boxes

Flyball boxes have come a long way in 25 years. They used to be a platform on the ground with a long arm attached that launched the ball when the dog stepped on the platform (picture a Chuckit attached to a shipping box – that's what it looked like). In fact, that's why it was called "flyball" to begin with – because the ball would fly up to ten feet in the air and the dog would have run to catch it.

These days flyball boxes are carefully crafted machines designed with the dog's optimum performance in mind. The ball is shot out by a mechanical launcher and the dogs are trained to turn on the box like a competition swimmer would turn on the wall in the pool (which is why we call it a **swimmer's turn** in flyball). If a dog's turn is good you will hardly even see him catch the ball before he has flipped around on the box and started back up the racing lane.

Thug is a six-year-old Border Collie x Staffordshire Bull Terrier mix owned by Russ Helganz of Ann Arbor, Michigan. Thug races with RPM Dog Sports and is seen here executing a beautiful swimmer's turn on an Eric Tindall flyball box. Thug's best time to date is a 3.61. Thug is apparently not a Thug - Russ says he's a sweet, gentle boy outside the ring, and calls him his "once in a lifetime" dog. (Photo by Len Silvester)

Flyball boxes are built for speed and safety. Box makers study hours of videotaped box turns and experiment with their box designs until they hit on a design that the dogs perform well on – the best angle, the right amount of padding, the best ball placement, the fastest and most accurate way to shoot out the ball.

Boxes are usually made out of painted wood, but you'll see a few designs that are made out of high density plastic or metal (I've even heard of one built out of aircraft-grade aluminum). All boxes have at least one layer of anti-fatigue matting (like Tuff-Spun) across the front surface so that dogs have a soft place to land. Most boxes also have some sort of no-slip surface on the bottom, too. You'll frequently see sandpaper attached to the bottom, or a section of clear plastic office chair matting (the kind with cleating), to keep the boxes from slipping around on the mats.

Relay (Stormfront's Squall Line) is a three-year-old Border Collie owned by Darlene Gottwald. He races with Synergy and typically runs in the 3.8's. He is showing off his awesome turn on a Synergy "SpringBack" style box made by Kevin Hesse.
(Photo by Len Silvester)

Advising you on what type of box to buy is tricky, especially if you are just getting into the sport and trying to keep your costs low. Boxes are big investments. The Premier box, built by Dan Phillips, is quite popular (and is endorsed by Spring Loaded, the NAFA Multibreed world record holders), but costs around $1300 with shipping. Eric Tindall and Norm Glover also make great wooden flyball boxes, and they cost about half the price of a Premier. There is usually a wait list for boxes since these guys make them in their spare time.

🐕 *Launchers on the inside of a Premier box.*

If you're starting your own club and you want to do it right, go ahead and invest in a good box. You'll regret it later if you don't. The boxes used by the competitive teams are just so well designed – they have the maximum size pedal for the dogs to turn on, great launching mechanisms that hold up with a lot of wear and tear, and the specs (e.g., where the holes are located) have been carefully plotted out based on a lot of research and testing.

You could also build your own box, if you're handy like that. Specs for flyball boxes are located in the NAFA and U-FLI rulebooks, so use those as your guide. U-FLI's rules allow for a slightly larger box – U-FLI's box dimensions are 30 inches wide x 20 inches tall x 30 inches deep while NAFA's are 24 inches wide x 18 inches high x 30 inches deep. Since many clubs compete in both organizations, most boxes you see used in competition will be the slightly smaller NAFA size.

Judges measure and inspect all the clubs' flyball boxes right before the tournament, so make sure whatever you build will pass inspection!

*Nova (Nataki's Super Nova) is a Border Collie x Jack Russell mix owned by Kathy Austin of Rochester, New York. Nova plays NAFA flyball with Buffalo Wings and U-FLI with Flyball Insanity of Ottawa and she is a height dog on both teams. She's seen here on a Dan Phillips Premier flyball box. **(Photo by Dave Strauss)***

Used flyball boxes go up for sale every once in a while, and clubs or individuals will generally post an announcement about it on one of the flyball email lists or Yahoo groups. You could also post an email to one of those lists yourself and ask if anybody has a box they'd like to sell.

If you're just getting started and you're not sure about how involved in flyball you'll be, you might be better off building a ramp out of plywood, then glue matting on top, and use Velcro to stick the ball in the right place on the board to simulate a flyball box (the standard fuzzy yellow-green tennis balls stick perfectly to Velcro). This is a great substitute for a few months while you're teaching your dog all the necessary skills. By then you will have hopefully hooked up with a local club and can use their box to practice on.

Some clubs have extra boxes that they are willing to loan out, so that's an option, too. When I moved down to North Carolina from Massachusetts, there were no clubs in my area and I had no equipment. Another club (Mike Randall's team Blockade Runners) loaned me one of their spare boxes for a few months while I got settled in the area and figured out what I wanted to do. They were three hours away from me so it didn't make sense for me to go practice with them every weekend, but borrowing their box helped me a lot.

Jumps

Flyball jumps are white 6-inch baseboards supported by uprights (called **stanchions**) on each side. The inside width of the baseboard is 24 inches and the uprights are somewhere between 24 inches and 36 inches tall. The uprights can be painted a different color (other than white) if your club wants to get a little fancy with their branding. A full set of flyball jumps is four baseboards, eight uprights, and a slew of different-sized slats (in 1-inch, 2-inch, and 4-inch increments) to add height to the baseboards as necessary.

Here you can see that the jump height is set to 8 inches - a 6-inch baseboard plus two 1-inch slats. **(Photo by Len Silvester)**

Jumps are pretty easy to get your hands on. You can build your own set out of a sheet of plywood (Google "flyball jump plans"), or you can buy pre-made sets from a variety of places online.

Exact specs for the jumps are also in the NAFA and U-FLI rulebooks.

If you make your own, be sure to really sand down the areas where the jumps fit together, otherwise when the wood expands you'll struggle to get them together or pull them apart every time you use them. Sand them nice and smooth all over, paint them white, and you're all set. I built a set one afternoon with my dad, and it wasn't too difficult.

Flyball jumps can also be made with Sintra, a type of hard PVC foam board. Sintra jumps are great because they're a little lighter than wood, nice and smooth on the edges, and can be left outside all the time (they don't warp, expand, or grow mold). You'll pay a lot more for these than plywood jumps, but they last forever. They also have more give to them than wood, which is good for safety reasons – if a dog plows into a Sintra jump, it will flex a little bit with the force. You may have to replace some of the 1-inch or 2-inch slats (they will snap if they are hit hard), but the safety benefit makes it worth the cost.

Props

A **prop** is a training aid that helps you make your dog more successful while he's learning flyball. The standard ones are:

Jump board in front of the box

This is probably the most common prop you'll see people using. It's usually half of a jump (the baseboard plus one stanchion), or two halves of two jumps put together, or a long custom made jump that sits right in front of the box to remind the dog to put their back feet up on the box.

My club likes to put a piece of foam across the top of the prop to prevent dogs from nicking their toes on it if they accidentally hit it – we use a kids' pool noodle (cut to the length of the prop) and just push it down on top of the plywood.

Many dogs never see the flyball box without a prop in front of it until they are competing. Props can't be used during the actual race, but they're permitted during warm-ups, so handlers will warm their dogs up with the prop in front of the box, and then pull it away right before the race starts.

🐕 *Lickety Split's jump board (and ball) ready to go for warm-ups.* **(Photo by Len Silvester)**

Most clubs paint (or tape) the last 6 inches of their flyball box's pedal white to simulate the look of a jump board in front of it – many competitors believe that this simple visual cue helps remind the dogs to get all four feet up on the box when the prop isn't there.

I'll explain more about this type of prop in the box training section of the book.

Ring gating

Gates are used in several ways:

- On either side of the jumps to keep the dog from running around them
- In between lanes to prevent a dog from crossing over to chase the dog running next to it
- Next to the box to remind the dog not to turn wide

The wooden or white plastic folding ring gates can be pretty expensive – $30 or so for one 5-foot section of gating plus the uprights.

If you just need a gate or two (to rein in a wide turn or remind a dog to take the jump after he turns off the box), go ahead and invest in the freestanding PVC folding ring gates. I have two of them and have gotten a lot of use out of them over the years – they are super light and fold right up for storage.

If you need gating that runs the entire length of the lane (to act as a jump tunnel for green dogs or to keep dogs from crossing over from one lane to the other), you can save a lot of money by getting creative. The dogs don't care what it looks like. Buy a roll or two of plastic garden fencing at Lowe's or Home Depot and figure out the best way to make it stand up – if you practice outside you can get some garden stakes and push them into the ground every 5 feet or so, then drape the fencing on top. If you practice on concrete and mats, you can fashion some sort of post out of wood or PVC pipe and secure it in a block of concrete as your base.

Other props

Different dogs need different props. Some just need a jump board in front of the box and that's it. Others practically require you to build a wall in front of the box so they can't put their feet anywhere except exactly where they're supposed to.

🐾 *This Wall o' Props was built to help this dog get his feet in the right place. He was "cheating" and not putting his back feet up on the box until the props in front of the box were wide enough to accommodate his long reach.*

Some dogs never skip a jump while others actively dodge them (especially Jack Russell Terriers – it's faster to run back when you skip the jumps, you know).

A lot of everyday objects can double as props, like a triangular Fed Ex tube or a short section of plastic rain gutter. These are good substitutes for a jump board if your dog just needs a gentle reminder to get all four feet up on the box, or they can be laid on the floor on either side of the box to remind the dog to run up the center of the lane.

Rewards and Toys

I'll cover this topic more in the training section, but rewards and toys are pretty much what flyball is all about. You want your dog to run down to the flyball box as fast as he can, get the ball, and then run back to you as fast as he can. So you need to have a really great reward waiting for him. Motivators will vary from dog to dog.

Some dogs will play with whatever their handler has in their hands – a ball, a tug, or a piece of plastic garden hose. Others will run best for food, or for a certain tug toy or floppy disc (like Booda's pink and green Soft Bite Floppy Discs), and some are so ball obsessed that they will only run for another ball (or they'll bring their ball to you so you can tug on it with them).

The rules state that you can't distract another team in any way during racing, so throwing balls or Frisbees is prohibited in the runback area. You also can't use squeaky toys because terriers will go nuts over stuff like that. But other than that, you can use pretty much anything as a motivator. I've seen people out in the lanes with giant stuffed animals, the above-mentioned garden hose, and a large bucket lined with Cheese Whiz (it was for a Jack Russell Terrier, and he would run into the cheesy bucket after every heat – this was also how they caught him).

My dogs come back for various things – fleece tugs, rope tugs, fur tugs, those pink and green floppy discs, or a tug pouch stuffed with cheese. I had a Jack Russell once who was so addicted to fetching that I used the Chuckit for her first several tournaments to remind her to bring the ball back to me (I didn't throw the ball with the Chuckit, I just let her bite the plastic handle in between heats).

Some competitors prefer not to use food and will do whatever it takes to switch their dogs over to a tug toy instead. I say do whatever works. Dogs are bred to perform a variety of jobs – hunting, herding, protection, or companionship – so different breeds are motivated by different things. Some dogs are REALLY motivated by food! But keep in mind that food requires a dog to stop in front of you, while coming back to a tug allows the dog to drive through to the end (some literally, as their handlers will swing them up into the air on the tug at the end of each heat). If you're using food, you may get better results if you run away from your dog with his food reward, and/or stand much farther in the runback area, that way he's not slowing down for the food while he's still powering through the flyball course.

🐾 *Border Collie Fun is having fun at the end of her tug. Fun is owned by Jay-Jay Rasing of Thornhill, Ontario, and races with Instant Replay.* **(Photo by Len Silvester)**

Try not to leave self-rewarding toys like balls and tugs lying around at home. Your dog should associate playing with these things *with* you. Instead of balls and toys, I have a bunch of those big natural beef bones and a few Kongs scattered around my living room to keep my dogs busy when they're in the house.

Collars and Harnesses

Choke collars, prong collars, bark collars, and e-collars are strictly prohibited in flyball. The best type to use is a simple buckle or clip collar, or, if your dog has a tendency to slip out of his collar, a martingale is great (that's the type of collar you'll often see on greyhounds). Martingales are different from choke collars because they only tighten up to a certain point – they keep the dog from slipping his head out of the collar, but don't choke him.

Some people really like to run their dogs in harnesses, especially if they have a hard-to-catch little dog or a hard-to-hold-onto big dog. If you use a harness, make sure it doesn't restrict your dog's movement at all and that it doesn't chafe his skin when he runs.

Also, remove all those jangling swinging dog tags from your dog's collar when he's racing, or use a tag pouch. I've seen some poor dogs trying to run all weekend while being hit in the face with their tags.

I run my dogs with just a light buckle/clip collar, even if they're hard to catch or hold onto. I think the more unencumbered they are, the faster they are. (You can even run them "naked" if you want, collars aren't required.)

Electronic Judging Systems

The Electronic Judging System (or Digital Scoring System, as it's called by U-FLI) is a sophisticated piece of equipment that tracks and displays start times, individual dog times, and overall team times to the thousandth of a second. The head judge and line judges also rely on it to let them know when there's an early pass – the dogs are moving so fast that it can be hard to see a bad pass with the naked eye. A red light will flash on at the top of the light tree when the incoming dog breaks the infrared beam before the returning dog does.

The EJS consists of:

- A tall light tree that stands between both lanes by the start/finish lines

- Infrared sensor panels at each team's start/finish line

🐑 *Lanes, EJS, and digital displays all set up and ready for the tournament.*

- A small control panel that sits on the scoring table
- Two large digital display screens that are usually set up near the boxes on the outside of the ring

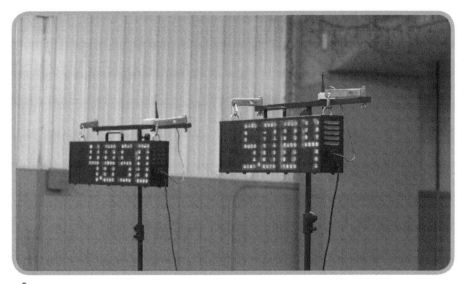

🐑 *Digital displays.* **(Photo by Dave Strauss)**

The digital display screens are recent additions – we started seeing them at tournaments in the mid 2000's. They display the start times (**reaction time**), individual dog times (**split times**), and final times as they're happening, making life easier for the competitors and the race more exciting for spectators.

NAFA and U-FLI provide clubs with an EJS system (or two, if there are enough teams entered) to use for their tournament weekend. Very few clubs own their own EJS (each system costs about $7,000).

Basic Skills for Dogs

Training with a Clicker or Verbal Marker (like "Yes")

Before I go into any of the specific skills your dog needs to play flyball, I want to take a few minutes to talk about training with a clicker or verbal marker.

Although this type of training is certainly not required to learn flyball, it works really well and can speed up the training process immensely. I use a clicker to train almost all the foundational flyball skills – recalls, targeting, the beginnings of the box turn, picking up a ball (if the dog doesn't like balls), standing for measuring, and drop it/out (for balls and tugs).

You can buy a clicker for a dollar or two at any pet store. It looks like a little plastic kid's toy and sounds sort of like a cricket.

Some people prefer not to mess with a clicker and will use the word "Yes" (or "Good" or something like that) instead – that's okay, too. I personally have better luck with the clicker, because I find it to be faster and more precise than me trying to say "Yes" at exactly the right time, but I'm also not the most coordinated person in the world.

In a nutshell, you use the clicker to mark (with the "click" sound it makes) exactly when your dog is doing something you like, and to let them know that a reward is coming. I think of it as a taking a picture – when I see what I want, I click (or use the mark word).

(Throughout the rest of the book, whenever I mention clicking or click/treating a dog's behavior, feel free to replace "click" with your verbal marker instead.)

Practice training in different places, because dogs tend to learn things in context (they'll sit beautifully in the kitchen next to the refrigerator, for example, but may look at you quizzically if you say "Sit" at the dog park). You'll definitely see this phenomenon during flyball training – dogs who love the tennis ball or who tug like maniacs at home may show zero interest in these things at flyball practice.

My Border Staffy Fringe, when she was two years old (she's four now), working for cheese sticks during a break in flyball practice.

You can also use every meal as a training session – when I'm really trying to get one of my dogs going on something, I'll put their kibble in a bowl, carry it out to the living room, and use a few pieces of kibble at a time for their reward while I'm working with the clicker.

If you've never worked with a clicker before, read Karen Pryor's book *Don't Shoot the Dog* or visit her website at http://www.clickertraining.com and watch some of the videos there. Pryor is one of the pioneers of clicker training and trained dolphins with clickers back in the 1960's before applying what she learned to dogs. Pat Miller's book *The Power of Positive Dog Training* is also a great read and explains clicker training very well.

Keeping it positive

Flyball is supposed to be *fun*. Dogs that love the game will run their hearts out every time they race. You want your dog to trust you and do his very best for you, so make all your training as positive as possible. Your dog should offer behaviors to you willingly and enthusiastically.

I try to ignore what my dog is doing wrong and focus on what he's doing right during training sessions. If my dog does something wrong (especially if it's a big Ooops, like crossing over to visit another dog early in his training), I may say, "Uh-oh! Let's try that again" (giving him no reward for what he just did wrong) and try the exercise again.

Some dogs may need a little "time-out" in their crate if they are having a really hard time paying attention to you. Don't get mad or frustrated, just end the activity, essentially teaching your dog, "If you don't listen, you don't play." You can work another dog instead for a few minutes, then try bringing him back out for another chance.

A couple of my dogs are so sensitive that even an "Uh-oh!" plus no reward is enough to make them to shut down (if you guessed "Border Collies!" you were right), so sometimes I just reward them by degrees – for instance, I will still tug a little bit with the dog that didn't do it quite right, but when he gets it totally right I will say "YES!!!!" and have a crazy tug party with him.

It's easier to keep things positive if you tweak the environment to set your dog up for success – use ring gating to keep him from running around the jumps, props to get his feet in the right place on the box, and don't rush any steps in his training. Make sure he knows what you're asking him to do, and that he's doing it for you consistently, before you progress to the next step.

Basic Obedience Skills

You don't really *need* the typical obedience commands in flyball – sit, down, stay – but they certainly don't hurt. For example, it is nice to be able to put your dog into a down-stay while you're setting up jump heights or something, but usually in the ring you're holding onto your dog for dear life while you wait to release him. A down-stay won't cut it in that type of environment, and frankly, I'm okay with that. I love to see my dogs all cranked up and ready to explode down the lane – it reminds me of the horses in the Kentucky Derby, ready to burst out of their starting boxes.

These dogs are CRANKED, and that's one of the things I love the most about flyball. This is Rocket Relay's "A" team, counting down to the start of the race. **(Photo by Marsha Lundy-Almond)**

A lot of people who play other dog sports frown on what looks like a bunch of ill-mannered dogs barking uncontrollably in the flyball lanes, but the truth is many flyball dogs have lovely manners and hold all sorts of obedience titles and therapy dog certifications. These dogs just know it's okay to let loose and have fun during flyball, just like kids know that they can run around and scream during recess but not during science class.

Dogs also seem to have no trouble transitioning from one sport to the other. They may compete in obedience one weekend, agility the next weekend, and flyball the next, and perform beautifully in all three competitions. It's all about context.

When you're competing in any dog sport, it is nice to have dogs that are:

- Happy and comfortable spending time in their crates (even better if you can also get them to stay in exercise pens, for the tournaments that have lots of crating room).

- Okay riding in the car on long trips.

- Good walking on a leash at rest areas, hotels, and tournament sites.

- Tolerant of other people touching them and other dogs approaching them.

Toy and Tug Drive

Although it's fine to train with food, most dogs will come back to you faster if there's something to interact and play with instead. Toys appeal to their natural prey drive. This is especially true of the higher-drive dogs – several of my dogs won't even look at food during flyball because they're so hyped up, and tugging gives them an outlet for this energy. Plus a tug is a really visible target, even when the dog is turning off the box and you're over 60 feet away in the runback area.

Handler Peter Russell is offering a perfectly-placed tug as a reward for three-year-old Border Collie Shayde (Rival's Sudden Blackout at Power Tripp). Peter and Shayde race with Buffalo Wings in New York. **(Photo by Dave Strauss)**

Some dogs are born tuggers and others need a bit more cajoling (especially if tugging was discouraged when they were puppies).

If you're patient and give it five minutes a day, you can build up a great tug drive in most dogs using the following formula:

- Choose the kind of motivator you want to use (based on what your dog seems to prefer) – a long fleece tug? A pink and green floppy disc? A stuffed animal? A treat pouch on a rope? Pick one toy and stick with it.

- Don't let your dog play with that toy/tug/motivator unless he is playing with you. (At my house, the only things left out for my dogs to free-play with are Kongs and bones. No tugs, no toys, no balls.)

- For the first day or two, put the motivator out of reach – I put mine up on the fireplace mantle. Tease the dog with it – throughout the day, pick it up off the mantle, say things like, "What have I got?" in a happy, excited voice, and play with it above your head, out of your dog's reach. Make your dog crazy to get to that motivator.

- Once your dog is very excited about the motivator, tease him with it within his reach. Let him chase after it or bite it a little bit. Make him work for it! Do not just hold the tug between your two hands and present it to your dog. Appeal to his natural desire to chase and bite things – make the toy come alive.

- Play keep-away and chase games with the motivator – keep them very brief and always leave your dog wanting more. I let my dogs chase me around the house (just one dog at a time!) after a tug or floppy disc, or I'll put the tug around my neck when we go for a walk, and when we get back to my yard I'll break into a sprint for the front door, dragging the tug behind me. The dogs go nuts for this stuff.

If your dog has a soft mouth or is tentative about taking the tug at first, just be patient. Play gently at first. Don't rip it out of his mouth. If you have a really reluctant dog on your hands, you can try tugging with another dog (preferably one who is a crazy tugger) in front of your dog. You can put your dog in a crate and tug with the other dog right in front of him. Then put the other dog away and bring your dog out while he's still excited and try again.

On the other end of the spectrum, if your dog gets too enthusiastic and accidentally nips your hand, don't make a big fuss out of it. Obviously it's not okay if the dog is biting your hands on purpose, but if he's just having a great time and gets a little carried away, no biggie. Wear gloves (Mechanix brand gloves are the bomb!).

Recalls

A good recall is arguably the most important skill in flyball. Sure, getting the ball is important, but you want your dog to run back to you as fast as he can *after* he gets the ball. You also want to be able to call your dog back to you if something weird happens (e.g., a bobbled ball or a dog in the other lane crossing over).

Plus a lot of flyball training in general is done off-lead and your dog is always working around other dogs, so a reliable recall is critical.

One way to build a great recall early on is to walk around with treats in your pocket and call your dog when he's not expecting it. My team likes to use the command "Here" after the dog's name (said in a loud but cheerful voice), like this: "Boomer, HERE!"

In the beginning, click/treat him when he glances your way after you call him. Work up to click/treating him for snapping his body around your way – you want to reward speed back to you.

When your dog is reliably coming to you in your house, move out to a fenced area and work on it there for a while. Once you feel confident that he's not going anywhere, move to a different location (move to your front yard if you've been working in your back yard, for example). Then start taking the show on the road. Take your dog to visit your friends and family, the park, and pet stores. Start introducing distractions on purpose – work on his recall around kids or another dog, and eventually in a small crowd of people. The ultimate test is being able to call him back to you during practice when there are other dogs running around and a lot going on.

You can mix it up by offering a toy as a reward instead of food. I prefer to de-emphasize the tennis ball, because I've had a few ball-obsessed dogs and it's a hard habit to break, so I'll play with a tug or a pink and green floppy disc with my dogs. I usually work with food for the first couple of weeks, and then switch over to the other reward once I know I have my dog's full attention. At home I still call my dogs randomly and surprise them with treats or a tug game. I want all of my dogs to believe that great things come from me, that when I call them they should hustle because they don't want to miss anything. (This also means you should not trick your dog and use "HERE!" to get him to come to you so you can clip his nails or put him in his crate. That's mean! Use different commands for that.)

Whatever you use as your reward, just be sure that you're fun and positive and keep sessions short and full of energy. After a while, your dog should practically be falling over himself to get to you when you call him.

Renowned dog trainer and agility competitor Susan Garrett has some great recall exercises you can do with your dog in her books (*Shaping Success* and *Ruff Love*) and on her blog at http://www.susangarrettdogagility.com.

Restrained recalls

Restrained recalls are one of the building blocks of flyball training. Actually, you never really stop doing them – many seasoned dogs with years of experience still do restrained recalls during tournament warm-ups to get them cranked up and also to remind them which lane they're running in.

For a restrained recall, somebody else holds your dog (usually by putting their hands around the dog's chest or hips, or holding the dog's collar or harness) while you run away from him. Then they let your dog go so he can chase you. When your dog reaches you, you do a lot of celebrating and play with him and/or give him treats.

Start out by doing this drill on the flat, then work up to one jump, then two, then three, then four. The eventual goal is to have somebody hold your dog at the flyball box and let your dog go so that he's running over the four hurdles and back to you in the runback area.

At first you may need to put up gates on either side of the jumps to keep your dog from running around them. Some trainers just run fencing along both sides of the lane, sort of like a tunnel, so there's no way the dog can make a mistake.

🐕 *Here's a dog being held for a restrained recall during practice. We also put a gate on either side of the first jump to guide the dog through the course.*

Here's the habit you are trying to create with all these recalls: during competition you want your dog to turn on the box, see you running away from him in the runback area, and put on the turbo speed to get back to you as fast as he can. The more exciting you are, the faster he is going to run.

Restrained recalls should be high energy and super-fun. Keep sessions short (5-8 reps) so that your dog doesn't tire out and get rewarded for running back to you slowly.

I never require my dog to sit in front of me when he comes to me for a recall – flyball is not obedience. Not that flyball and obedience are mutually exclusive, because they're not, but I am emphasizing drive and speed in flyball. I am usually running away from the dog, encouraging him to chase me, and then playing a great game of tug with him as a reward.

You can add variations to the restrained recall drill to make your dog run faster, like having another person run next to him up the lane (just as peripheral movement – they don't need to interact with him) or letting your dog chase another dog (preferably an experienced flyball dog) up the lane of jumps towards the handlers in the runback area. Make sure you leave a jump or two's worth of space in between the dogs, because you don't want your dog to actually catch the dog in front of him. The dog he's chasing should be very fast and exciting. Also, don't do this drill if your dog is a problem chaser – you don't want to create or reinforce bad habits. The chase recall drill is great for a dog that will reliably run to his handler for his reward and not chase the other dog around in the runback area, and it's especially good for dogs who just haven't been all that excited about recalls in the past. Adding another dog to the mix really livens things up.

Chase recall drill during a training workshop. The second dog (the Mini Aussie) was let go once the first dog (black dog leaving the box) was halfway up the lane (around the second jump).

We've done the chase drill in practices with three dogs at a time. The handlers bring their dogs to the holders down by the box, then run up the side of the jumps and call the dogs. When the handlers are far enough away (usually right before they reach the start/finish line), the holder of the first dog lets him go over the jumps. When the first dog has cleared the first jump, the second dog is let go, and so on. All the handlers play for a minute or two in the runback area with their dogs, then bring their dogs back down to the box for another round. The dogs love this drill.

It's a really good idea to start running your dog next to another dog as soon as possible – even better if you are training a puppy because they often haven't developed any bad habits yet. You can head off a lot of chasing issues if you desensitize your dog to motion in the other lane early on in his training. If you're worried that your dog might chase the other dog, just put up fencing in between the lanes, or have a line of people stand in between to act as blockers, gradually fading out the barrier over time.

Retrieving and Catching Balls

If you're lucky enough to have a dog that loves to fetch and can catch any ball that you throw at him, just move right along to the next section.

For a long time I thought all dogs liked balls, until I ended up with one, a Border Collie named Kraken, that had no interest in balls whatsoever.

My solution was to clicker train Kraken to retrieve balls and bring them back to me. I won't lie – this was a long, sometimes tedious process. But if you want to play flyball, the dog's gotta go get the ball.

I broke down the ball retrieval process into a series of small steps and used the clicker to shape the overall behavior one step at a time.

I started by rolling a tennis ball across the floor. Since it was moving, Kraken watched it roll by and I clicked/treated him for looking. After a few sessions of this, I could count on him to look at the ball, even when it wasn't moving. Eventually I worked up to having him walk over to the ball on his own, then pick it up in his mouth briefly.

He stayed with my friend, Barb, one weekend while I was out of town, and she took it to the next level by refrigerating the ball overnight in a Ziploc bag full of smelly chicken treats, then bringing it out to play with him the next day. She blocked off a long section of hallway in her house and rolled the ball down the hallway for him, clicking/treating him when he brought it back to her.

From there he was interested enough in the ball that I started loading it into the flyball box for him (he already had a nice swimmer's turn without the ball). At first the ball would just shoot out and either hit him in the head or sail right past him, but in time he would at least make the attempt to catch it. I switched to a squishy foam ball so that he just had to get a few teeth on it to be successful – this helped a lot, because catching a lot more meant he was getting rewarded a lot more, and from there he started associating the reward with getting his ball.

A fellow trainer had great success getting her Border Collie to hold onto his ball just by taking him outside to play fetch a lot. She put his tug away for several weeks and turned the ball into a high-reward toy – she didn't use a clicker or commands because she was worried that he'd think too much about it (which would slow him down in competition), she just wanted him to have fun. And he did. This new love for the ball carried over into the flyball lanes and pretty soon he was no longer spitting out his ball before he crossed the finish line.

Catching balls

If your dog likes balls but can't seem to catch one to save his life, try practicing at home with plain popcorn. Popcorn doesn't move that fast and you can practice with a lot at a time. Plus it tastes good – it's the ultimate reward for catching.

Balls shoot out of the box pretty fast, right at the dog's head, so at home you can practice catching by gently lobbing a ball at the dog's face from several feet away to get him used to having a ball fly right at his mouth. Use a soft foam ball if your dog is sensitive.

Ball Obsession

Once you realize you have a ball-obsessed dog, you need to go to work quickly to make a different motivator (tug, toy, floppy disc) the best thing in the whole wide world before you do any work with the ball – you don't even want to look at or acknowledge the ball until your dog is totally in love with his tug or toy. Five minutes a day a few times a week playing with the tug will go a long way toward this. Refer to the "Toy and Tug Drive" section earlier in this chapter.

Once your dog is addicted to his toy/tug, you can start reintroducing the ball by putting a **dead ball** (a ball that's not moving) on the ground near him while you're playing a game of tug with him. You may have to do this with him on a leash at first if he has the tendency to blow you off and go after the ball. Just stand there and wait him out if you have to, and only come alive again if he chooses to tug with you.

Once your dog will ignore a dead ball (or you can at least call him off of it easily), start kicking the ball around or tossing it a bit and while tugging with the motivator, until he's desensitized to the ball enough that he'll ignore it while tugging with you no matter what you do with the ball.

It's best not to do any box work with a ball until the ball obsession has been fixed, otherwise your dog's turn could fall apart – he'll be so interested in the ball that he may hang on the box too long or contort his body in strange ways when he turns, and/or he'll run a few steps down the face of the box versus launching off it because he's already gotten his "reward" (the ball) so in his mind there's no need for him to run back quickly to you now.

If you have a ball-obsessed dog, the ball should never be used as a toy at home – it should only be an object that earns a better motivator (the real reward, playing with you). Easier said than done, I know. For some dogs the ball is self-rewarding because it rolls around on its own and imitates prey and your dog doesn't need anybody to play with it with him...he can roll it around and toss it to himself. So you just have to make tugging with you *even more fun*. If you nip ball obsession in the bud early you can fix it.

If your dog really loves food, you could also try clicker training him to drop the ball on command for food, so that he understands what it means to pick up the ball on command and drop the ball on command. It's sort of like how when you teach dogs to "speak" it's then easier to teach them to be "quiet" because there's a command to their voice now, on and off. So you can teach him "get it" to pick it up (that one should be easy) and "drop it" to spit it out – stand there and wait him out if he won't drop the ball, and put him on a leash if necessary so he won't run away with it. He will finally spit it, especially if he really loves food and you're teasing him with something like hot dogs, and then you click/treat him with a big jackpot. Once he is consistently spitting for food you can switch over to having him drop it for the tug/toy reward instead.

Targeting

Targeting is a great way to teach your dog a flyball box turn (and it also comes in handy when you're teaching your dog non-flyball related tricks).

You can either teach a dog to touch a target stick with his nose/mouth, or teach him to touch a small target (like a plastic margarine top) with his front paw. I prefer the target stick but I know some people play other dog sports and want to emphasize that their dog touch something with their feet (like contacts for agility).

Touch stick

You can easily make your own touch stick with a skinny piece of white PVC pipe or a wooden dowel. You can find PVC pipe at Lowe's or Home Depot and ask them to cut it for you there. Mine is about 3 feet long, with a ¾-inch diameter.

I wrap the bottom of the touch stick with duct tape (just about 3 inches or so, to make a visual target), then rub a little cheese or peanut butter on the tape to make it smell good. When you bring your dog out to work and show him the touch stick, he's automatically going to sniff the end of the stick because it smells awesome. Click and treat him for touching the stick with his nose. It won't take any time at all before he's going nuts for that touch stick.

Start pointing the stick around at various things – on the couch, on the ottoman, on a chair, on the floor in different rooms, outside on the ground, etc.

Once your dog is offering the behavior to you on his own, add the "Touch" cue (or "Target" or something like that). Wait until your dog knows what you're asking for before you add the command. If you're new to clicker training, I know it feels weird to not give a command at first, but in the beginning the dog doesn't know what you're asking for so the word won't mean anything.

When you have a really reliable touch, you can start working with your dog on the ramp/wall/flyball box (covered later in this book).

Target

I first learned this type of targeting in beginner's agility class. Lots of flyball trainers use it, too.

You start out by making a little target – I love to use those small yellow plastic margarine tops (3 ½ inches in diameter), but you can also make a little target out of cardboard and masking tape or duct tape.

Cut up some really tasty treats – little pieces of hotdog or cheese work great for this. Put the treat in between your thumb and the bottom of the target.

Ignore your dog when he sniffs the target – you are waiting for him to touch it with his paw (at least one of them). You can help him out at first by holding the target on the ground (with your thumb and the treat under it) until he paws at it or accidentally steps on it with his foot. Click and treat when his foot makes contact.

This type of targeting usually takes a little longer to train than the touch stick, simply because it's natural impulse for the dog to put his nose on the touch stick, while touching the target with a foot takes a little shaping.

If he's really not getting it, try just putting the treat in your hand until he scratches that – reward that and gradually add the target back into the equation.

Once your dog is touching his foot to the target reliably, start moving the target around your house. Use a piece of tape folded up on the back to stick it to the couch, fireplace, or wall.

Now you're ready for the ramp/wall/flyball box.

Box Turns

A great box turn can be tough to train, but it makes all the difference in the world when it comes to speed and safety.

A few years ago, most flyball trainers were happy when their dogs ran down the box, triggered the box to get their ball, and brought it back. They weren't concerned so much with *how* the dog triggered the box and got the ball, as long as the dog ran consistently all weekend and didn't make any mistakes.

The trend in recent years has been to take the time to train a really great box turn. It takes a lot more work than the old way of just making sure your dog got the ball and came back, but the result is a much faster dog. A neat, efficient turn is also much safer and easier on the dog's body than a smash-and-grab type of turn.

This handsome young man with the beautiful box turn is Psycho, a four-year-old Border Collie owned by Colleen Morita. He races with X Flyball in Southern California. **(Photo by Todd V. Minnella)**

Most flyball injuries occur because of some sort of collision accident (and thankfully those are pretty rare), not because of a poor box turn. But if you watch a poorly-executed box turn on slow-motion video, or see an action shot of one captured by a photographer at a tournament, you'll cringe at the way some dogs hit the box.

What's a Good Box Turn?

Before you start training the box turn, you need to understand what makes a good one.

Foot placement is important. Let's say your dog turns to the left, so the ball will be in the upper left hand corner of the box. Now imagine the pedal of the flyball box is like the face of a clock. You want your dog to launch onto the pedal of the box with his front feet at around 10 o'clock then follow up with his back feet around 2 o'clock (toward the center of the box is fine). The actual placement will vary depending on the size of your dog and how flexible he is.

You also want your dog to approach the box at an angle, versus driving straight into it at top speed.

🐕 *Zoya is a six-year-old mix (thought to be Whippet x Shepherd) who was rescued from the Mat-Su Animal Shelter in Palmer, Alaska. She now races with Alaska Dogs Gone Wild and is handled by Stacy and Curtis Smith's eight-year-old daughter, Mesa. In this photo you can see what a nice efficient box turn looks like in action.*
(Photo by Dave Strauss)

Your dog's mouth should be close enough to the ball so that when he triggers the box, the ball shoots right into his mouth. You can increase or decrease the speed of many boxes by adjusting the trigger pressure, just remember that it needs to be set at a speed that works for all the dogs on the team (if you're going to use it in a tournament). For really fast dogs, the box should almost have a **hair trigger** on it, meaning you want to adjust it to the point where if you put your finger anywhere on the face of the pedal, the ball will fire out.

Your dog should push off of the box so that he's flipping around almost 180 degrees and landing near the center of the lane. The more motivated your dog is to get back to you, the easier time you will have teaching this last part. You want the dog to be popping off the box as fast as possible to get back up the lane to you in the runback area.

How to Determine Which Way Your Dog Turns

It's important to figure out which direction your dog turns naturally. Most dogs turn to their right (just like most people are right-handed), but you want to make sure before you start box work.

Hold your dog while you toss a ball (or a tug or a toy) about 10-15 feet away from him. Wait until the ball stops rolling, make sure he's centered as he's facing it, then send him after it. Which way does he turn when he picks up the ball and brings it back to you? Does he loop around to the right or to the left?

Another way to tell which way your dog turns is to teach him a "spin" command in both directions (I teach this with a combination of clicker training and luring the dog with food). Usually one direction comes really easily to the dog and one direction seems awkward.

Your dog's dominant side should become pretty clear after just a few repetitions. If you really can't tell a difference or your dog consistently mixes it up – turning 50 percent one way and 50 percent the other way – go ahead and train him to turn to the right, since that's the dominant side for most dogs.

Building the Right Muscle Memory

Start out your box training by doing lots of close-up work, so the dog's reward is just out of reach when he's turning on the box, then work up to longer distances over many training sessions (this is where all your restrained recall work pays off, too). Dogs tend to get sloppier when they're faster (from increased momentum), so a lot of close-up work is critical to build good habits for approach into the box and foot placement on the box.

Remember that you are building muscle memory in your dog as you train his box turn. It's just like a person learning how to swing a golf club, shoot a gun or dance a complicated series of dance steps – if you learn to do it right the first time, it's efficient and feels natural. If you have to start over after many reps of doing it the wrong way, it feels awkward and you tend to want to revert back to your old way of doing it, even if it's less efficient.

There's a book called *Motor Learning and Performance* by Dr. Richard Schmidt that discusses human muscle memory retention. According to Dr. Schmidt, it takes 300-500 poor movement patterns to create a faulty motor memory and 3,000-5,000 good quality movements to unwind it. So if you translate that to box turns: it'll take about 300-500 reps for a bad box turn to become muscle memory, and 3,000-5,000 good box turns to fix it. Gah! So do it right the first time!

There are a lot of different ways to train a box turn. I'll explain three different methods in detail later in this chapter, and you can also find a lot of examples and information on the web, especially YouTube (http://www.youtube.com). Every dog is different, so pick the training method you feel the most comfortable with and go from there.

At this point in my flyball training, I start doing a lot of videotaping. It's hard to be coordinated with your treats and clicker and target stick *and* try to watch exactly where your dog is landing, what he's looking at, and how he's pushing off the ramp/wall/box. A lot of smartphones and digital cameras come with a video setting these days, so you probably won't have to buy any fancy equipment. I use my phone to videotape short training sessions (one or two minutes at a time), then play the video back on my computer so I can review the training session and tweak things accordingly the next time around.

Three Different Box Training Methods

Method #1: Touch stick and ramp/wall

This is the training method I'm currently using with my dogs, although all the methods I explain below are used by top teams and have produced good box turns.

The Ramp

You'll need to build yourself a ramp for this method, but it's cheap and easy. You just need a piece of plywood that's bigger than the face of the flyball box (a 4-foot by 4-foot piece is perfect), with some rubber matting glued onto it so that your dog has a soft place to land. You can buy matting by the foot at Lowe's or Home Depot, and there are some great spray adhesives (3M makes one) that will attach the matting to the box with minimal effort and mess.

You can lean your ramp up against a wall or object, just make sure that it can't slide around at all when the dog jumps on it. My ramp is actually attached to a stand and hinged so that it's stable and adjustable.

The ramp is an easy starting point for the dog – you can make the angle very gentle, almost like a table for them to jump on and off of, and then increase the angle as you go (sometimes this is necessary if you have a tentative dog).

By now, your dog should already know what "Touch" means and he will follow the touch stick wherever you point it. Stand on the right hand side of the ramp (if your dog turns to the right) and point at the center of the ramp with the stick and say "Touch." (Note: If you don't want to use a touch stick, you can also use a tug to lure the dog on and off the ramp. The touch stick usually works better, though, because it acts like a long extension of your arm. This lets you stand farther back from the ramp and get into position really fast, which will create a better turn for your dog.)

🐕 *Here's a great example of a ramp. This one happens to be leaning up against the box (it was being used in a drill with a big Malinois who was having trouble getting all his feet on the box - the ramp gave him more room to put his feet and built up his confidence). This ramp could easily be moved away from the box, though, and used alone (it has a stand on the back that folds out).*

It's important to whip the touch stick off the ramp really fast. You don't want your dog to hang out there on the ramp sniffing the touch stick. You want him to snap on and off the ramp very quickly. Also, whip the end of the stick off towards the center of the lane as he's jumping onto the ramp so that he doesn't get into the habit of turning wide over to the right to get his reward from you.

Make sure that all four of your dog's feet get up onto the ramp – you may need to put a jump board prop in front of the ramp to ensure that he doesn't just put two feet on it.

Once your dog is doing nice snappy turns off the ramp, you can move to the wall.

The Wall

You could move directly from the ramp to the flyball box, but I like doing wall work because it encourages the dogs to get up high (your ultimate goal is for them to have a nice high box turn with all four feet up) and it increases their rear-end awareness. Since the wall is vertical, they have to use their back feet to push off. They can't cheat on the wall!

They should be getting up there pretty high – one way to determine foot placement is to gently take your dog's front paws (so he's standing on just his back legs) and place them against the wall. You don't have to stretch his front legs out, just place his feet where they'd rest naturally if he put them up there himself. Then put a pencil mark or piece of tape on the wall at his elbows – that's how high your dog's front and back feet should be getting when he's pushing off with them.

Don't ever use a prop in front of the wall. This point has been driven home to me by some really great trainers – if your dog doesn't have enough momentum and slides down the wall instead of launching off it, he could hit the prop with his leg or knee and injure himself. Even if it didn't hurt him physically it could freak him out a little bit mentally.

If your dog turns to the right, you'll hold the touch stick in your right hand and a tug (or whatever toy he loves) in your left hand, then follow these steps:

❶ Start by holding the tip of the stick against the wall (high up, where you want your dog's head to aim).

❷ Say your "touch" command.

❸ As your dog's front feet are hitting the wall, whip the touch stick back to the center of the mat behind him and say "Here!" at the same time.

❹ Reward your dog with the tug in your left hand.

Ideally, your dog will be landing in about the same spot he took off from – the goal is a 180-degree rotation.

You won't need to move a lot during this exercise (although the coordination is a little tricky at first). It should just be a matter of whipping the stick off with your right hand and taking one step IN and back, toward the center of the lane and away from the wall. (If you have a big powerful dog you might need to take an additional step or two.)

🐕 *This is Barb Walton working with her Border Collie, Twyst Moy, on the wall. This photo was taken in 2007 - Barb is one of the first people I know who trained her dog using the wall method, and the result was a really great four-footed box turn and consistent 3.9-second times (and Twyst is a big leggy boy, he stands close to 22" tall at the shoulders). Wall training has evolved a bit since 2007, so the one thing we'd do differently now (from this photo) is to whip the touch stick off the wall and towards the grass as soon as the dog's front feet hit the wall.*

If your dog just doesn't get the concept of the wall or is nervous about it, go back to the ramp for some more work – increase the angle on the ramp over time until it is practically vertical like a wall. Make the reward really exciting and fun. Then come back to the wall and try again.

Once you are getting a really nice quick turn off the wall, it's time to move to the box.

The Box

Now the real fun begins – you're finally on the box! This step should actually be easy for your dog if you've put the time into the ramp and the wall. By now, this turning stuff should be old hat.

If you don't have a box of your own, you can keep working on the ramp (at about a 45-degree angle). When it comes time to introduce the ball (more on that below), you can Velcro a ball to the ramp in the appropriate place and start working on your dog's head placement. When you get a chance to work on a real box at practice, your dog should be practically trained already.

Dogs who have been working on the ramp and the wall usually don't think twice about leaping onto the box – it's just a variation on what they've already been doing all this time. The one thing new about the box is the sound it makes when it triggers (some are quiet but others can make a pretty loud "POW!" sound). Before you start doing box work, trigger the box a few times to make sure your dog isn't afraid of it. If he is, you may need to spend a few sessions desensitizing him to the noise (some trainers like to leave the box sitting in their house and feed their dog on it to make him really comfortable around it). You can also wrap a towel around the launcher on the inside of the box to muffle the sound for a few sessions if you need to.

Work on the box the way you've been working on the ramp and wall. Make sure you use a prop in front of the box at all times. Also make sure that the box isn't moving around at all – you want your dog to be totally confident that the box is not going to rock or move when he hits it. When I'm working with one of my dogs at home and don't have another person who can stand behind the box, I'll push it up against the wall and wedge an upside-down hurdle with stanchions behind it – it doesn't budge.

Transition from the touch stick to a verbal command and start using whatever reward will get your dog moving off the box at top speed (most of my dogs love food but they REALLY love tugs or floppy discs and will pop off the box much faster for them). Ditching the touch stick will free you up to move more quickly into the center of the lane with the reward, encouraging a tighter turn.

🐕 *This is my Border Collie, Kraken Moy, learning his box turn in 2008. I included it here because the whole set-up looks great in terms of prop placement, where his feet are on the box, etc., but I want to point out that I am way too close to him in this photo. I should have been several feet further up the lane, with the tug hanging down right into the center of the mat. (If your dog is too fast for you, you can get somebody else to let him go for you so you can be where you need to be when he pushes off the box.)*

Videotape the sessions to make sure your dog has good foot placement and that he's turning tightly into the center of the lane. Whenever I review videotape I see all sorts of little things that could be improved upon (usually they are due to crappy handling on my part – I'm not fast enough or exciting enough, I'm causing the dog to turn wide by the way I'm standing, etc.).

Method #2: Target and ramp/wall

This is the training method I used 8-10 years ago to train several of my dogs, and they all ended up with nice turns. I like the touch stick a little better than the target because the touch stick feels like an extension of my finger/hand/arm and I like the idea of being able to "point" to something. But the target is also a great way to teach your dog the box.

Basically, you're going to follow the same steps as you would in Method #1, just replacing the touch stick with the target. Instead of pointing to the ramp/wall/box with the touch stick, you're going to tape the target to the ramp, then to the wall, then to the box.

Put the target where you'd like the dog's *front feet* to hit.

If you've been using a target like a plastic margarine top or a small piece of cardboard, you can transition from this to an "X" made out of two pieces of masking tape – this works great if the dog keeps knocking the target off the box with his feet. Start out by taping the target to the box with X-shaped masking or duct tape, then eventually remove the target and just put the taped "X" up there by itself.

Method #3: Over prop to box method

This is the method we used to train the dogs in our beginner flyball class. It works great for all sizes and shapes of dogs, and is particularly good for timid or distracted dogs. It's also easy for the human students to understand and master. The other nice thing about this method is that it incorporates teaching the dog to jump over a hurdle, and gets him accustomed to a prop in front of the box at the same time.

Instead of a single jump (6-inch base with two stanchions) I like to start out with a longer jump to give the dog and handler more room to move around, so I will take two halves of two jumps and put them together.

You can also start out with a FedEx tube or a piece of plastic rain gutter instead of a jump, especially if you're working with a small dog.

Stand to the side of the jump (on whichever side your dog turns) and lure your dog back and forth over it with food or a toy, eventually assigning the command "Over".

Make sure your dog is moving fast – you want to lure him over the jump in one direction then quickly lure him back over the jump in the opposite direction so that he's pivoting on the floor and pushing off fast over the jump after his reward.

Start out with the jump 10-15 feet away from a flyball box (or ramp) and eventually (over several sessions) move the jump closer and closer to the flyball box, until the jump is very close to the box and it becomes your dog's natural tendency to push off the front of the box instead of the floor as he goes over the jump after his reward.

After a few sessions you should be able to stand next to the flyball box (on the right-hand side if your dog turns to the right – acting sort of like a human stanchion) and use your toy or food reward to lure your dog quickly on and off the box (over the jump, which is now right in front of the box acting like a prop).

If your dog is catching the tug or food at the box, or getting so distracted by the reward that his turn is falling apart (he's crashing into the prop or falling off the edge of the box), there are several things you can try:

- Move away faster with the reward

- Have somebody else hold his reward farther back in the lane

- Toss the reward down the lane a bit.

Your goal is to get him to snap off the box into the center of the lane.

If Your Dog Will Not Put His Back Feet on the Box

Sometimes, with any of the above box training methods, you'll get a dog who just will not put his back feet up on the ramp/wall/box. Either he doesn't understand what you want, or he has no rear-end awareness (a lot of dogs seem to think their bodies stop at their shoulders!), or he's nervous about putting his back feet up there.

There's a good exercise you can use to get over this hump. It's a little tricky from a coordination standpoint and you may end up feeling like a human pretzel, but it's amazing how well it works.

Let's assume your dog turns to the right. Before you start, put a jump board prop in front of the box (about a foot away from it). Then follow these steps:

❶ Put the outside of your left foot against the box and stand sideways so that your body's facing toward the right side of the box. Your dog will be behind you in the lane.

❷ Twist to the left (towards the box) and look behind you at your dog. Lure him around your leg onto the box with food or a toy. He needs to jump over the prop in order to do this, so you may need to fiddle with prop and foot placement (you could put the prop right against the box and put your foot against the prop instead). I know it sounds confusing – look at the photos for help.

❸ Move quickly towards the center of the lane to snap your dog off the box, then reward him with his food or toy.

🐕 *Here's a view of this exercise from two different angles. Don't worry about exactly where the dog's feet are touching yet - the goal here is to get the dog feeling comfortable putting his feet up on the box and pushing off the box.*

In this exercise, your body is a natural barrier – standing in front of the box and luring your dog around you forces him to put all four feet up on the box. There's no other place for his back feet to go. He's comfortable being close to your body so he'll curve himself around you to get the reward, putting his front feet and back feet on the box in the process. Praise him big-time for this – it's usually a big breakthrough when he gets it.

Once your dog is comfortable putting all his feet up on the box, lure him around your leg and start tossing his reward a few feet away from you into the center of the lane – this will encourage him to snap off the box past your body and get him used to pushing off with his back legs.

It should only take another session or two before you can move from the front of the box over to the right-hand side of the box – your dog should be able to pop on and off the box on his own, without going around your body.

Adding the Ball

Once your dog has a nice snappy four-footed turn on the box, it's time to add the ball. Don't wait too long to introduce the ball, otherwise your dog could get too comfortable turning without one (and this usually means his head position will be all wrong, because he has no ball to focus on). Start out by releasing him from about ten feet away from the box. This will give him enough space to build up speed and momentum, but it's still close enough for good control.

Try loading the ball to see if he will catch it – some dogs are just naturals at this and catch it from day one. If your dog is struggling to catch the ball or ignoring it altogether, start with a "dead" ball – one that just sits there in the hole or is attached to the box, ripe for the taking. Some flyball boxes have recessed holes that the ball can sit in whether the trigger is loaded or unloaded – if yours is like this, great (but make sure the ball doesn't sit so far down in the hole that the dog can't steal it out of the box). If you can't put a ball into the hole without cocking the trigger mechanism, use Velcro instead. Fuzzy tennis balls stick great to heavy duty Velcro (buy the black industrial kind, you can find it pretty much anywhere). Stick a piece of Velcro right where the ball would normally be loaded into the hole. If there's literally a gaping hole there even when the box isn't loaded, put the Velcro as close to the hole as possible, preferably right above it because the ball will droop down a little bit. Some boxes have a handy little shelf directly under the holes that you can use instead of Velcro. You'll just have to assess the box you have and see what the best solution is.

Many boxes also let you slow down the launcher speed so that the ball shoots out slower than usual. You can also try using one of the training tennis balls or a squishy foam ball instead of a regular tennis ball to make it easier to catch.

If your dog is ignoring the ball, you may need to play with him and the ball a little bit beforehand. Roll the ball for your dog a few times until he's engaged, then pick the ball up, walk straight to the box, and put it in the hole (or on the Velcro or on the shelf) – then excitedly tell him to get his ball.

Most dogs' turns fall apart when you first introduce the ball, so don't panic if the beautiful swimmer's turn you spent so much time working on suddenly looks like a train wreck. Your dog has to change his head position to catch the ball (and his mental focus, as well), so it'll take a little while for him to adjust. But if you've built a good foundation with your box training by always using a prop, requiring your dog to put all four feet on the box, and making your reward exciting enough for him to snap off, his turn should clean up quickly.

This would be another good time to videotape to see if your dog is having any trouble with anything – you may decide to switch to a foam ball or slow your box launcher's speed down based on what you see.

Alternate between a loaded and unloaded ball until your dog is consistently catching a loaded ball. At that point, you can start backing him up and adding in a jump (the first jump is always 15 feet away from the box).

Phasing Out Props

Although it's important to use a prop in front of the box during training and practice, you also want to teach your dog that he should do the same pretty box turn every time, regardless of whether the prop is in or not.

Try taking the prop out at random times (for example, have the dog do two box turns with the prop in, then take the prop out for the third turn) and reward the dog for each nice turn. You can also click or verbally mark when the dog is doing his nice turn so that he understands what he's being rewarded for.

Advanced Skills for Dogs

Jumps

Jumps are usually pretty easy and quick to train, especially if you do recalls with fencing or baby gates next to the jumps. Start out by doing a recall over one jump (use the jump closest to the box as your first jump) until your dog is taking that jump consistently, then add one jump at a time until you work up to all four jumps. As your dog is going over the jump say "Over!" to build an association between that word and that action.

Lucy is a scenthound mix owned by Lisa Routhier. She was rescued from the local humane society. She's seen here racing with Doggone Ballistic at Dogzworth's "Big O" tournament at Montreal's Olympic Stadium in November 2008. **(Photo by Len Silvester)**

You can really solidify this command at home by clicker training your dog to jump a hurdle (or anything, really – a Fed Ex tube or piece of gutter will do) and using the word "Over".

Start out training with low jumps at first. A 6-inch baseboard jump is fine for adult dogs and older pups. Younger pups should use something lower, like plastic rain gutters or even just slats on the ground.

Once your dog is doing recalls over four jumps and has a nice box turn, start adding jumps to his box work. Begin by doing a jump-box-jump drill, where you start your dog about 5-10 feet behind the jump closest to the box (which is 15 feet away from the box) and send him down to the box, then call him back over the jump to you. You can put gates up on either side of the jump to remind your dog not to go around it.

Once your dog has the hang of jump-box-jump, add in a second jump. So jump-jump-box-jump-jump. Make sure the dog is holding his nice turn and taking the jumps consistently before you add in the next jump. It shouldn't take long at all – just a few sessions, probably – before your dog is running the whole course.

Single striding

Most dogs, with the exception of the really small ones or the low-riders (like Bassett Hounds and Corgis), should be able to "single stride," meaning they only touch down once in between each jump. In flyball, the jumps are always set 10 feet apart from each other on the course.

Single striding is a much faster, more efficient way of running the course. All of my Jack Russell Terriers were able to single stride over their own NAFA jump height (even my little 13-inch-tall female), so if your dog has good structure and long legs (proportional to his height), he should be able to do it.

Some dogs don't single stride because they don't have enough speed/momentum to really power through the jumps. It's sort of like you running up the stairs two at a time – you can do it if you're moving fast enough and have enough forward momentum to propel you along. So sometimes it's just a matter of getting your dog more motivated to run to you (their handler, the most fun person on earth, remember?). Other times dogs just need a little time to get used to the jump placement and find their striding rhythm.

Passing Another Dog

No matter where your dog is in the lineup, he's going to have to pass somebody coming or going or both.

🐕 *Nice close pass at the start/finish line and the dogs look very comfortable.*
(Photo by Dave Strauss)

Many green dogs get so caught up in the game that they don't even notice another dog blasting by them, but others are really sensitive about their personal space and get easily distracted by another dog in the runback area.

To get your dog used to passing another dog, start out by having an experienced dog and handler hang out in the runback area while your dog is doing recalls. Have the other dog/handler start pretty far back at first, then gradually move up a few feet at a time until they are standing in lineup position (on the right side of the lane) while your dog runs by for a recall and his reward. It may take several sessions before your dog is comfortable with the other dog/handler standing there – that's okay. Don't rush him.

Next have the other handler send his dog down to the box for a full run once your dog is back from his recall and safely under your control (tugging and focused on you).

Then have the dogs switch places so that the other dog does a full run or a recall while your dog is being held in the runback area. Once your dog seems comfortable with this, start letting him go for a full run after the first dog runs by him – make sure you know your dog's full attention is down at the box before you let him go.

If you're having trouble getting your dog to focus down on the box, have another person run alongside him to get him revved up and get his attention where it needs to be. You can also have somebody stand down at the box and clap for your dog and call his name (sometimes it takes the box loader plus an additional person down there making a lot of noise to get your dog's attention). Don't talk to your dog while they're calling him – let the box loader or other person down at the box be the most exciting person at that moment.

Eventually you will be able to do full runs with both dogs passing each other. Be sure to alternate positions so that sometimes your dog is the start dog and sometimes he's the second dog.

Your dog will make quick progress, but be really conservative at first about how close you pass him with another dog. Start out with both dogs far apart and only tighten up the pass a foot or so each time. If you see your dog getting uncomfortable or distracted, move back to the last place he was comfortable and do a lot of reps at this distance until you think he's ready to move on.

It's really important that your partners in this drill are a seasoned dog and handler pair – the other handler needs to be able to recognize when it's safe to let their dog go, and their dog needs to be really solid and confident so that they'll totally ignore your dog if he does something silly like growls, barks, or chases.

Your dog will care less and less about other dogs as he gets more excited about flyball and more accustomed to others being in the runback area with him.

Lane hogs and swervers

If you have a dog that hogs the center of the lane, making it difficult for another dog to pass him, you need to find a way to push him over to the correct side of the lane (to the right if he's heading down to the box and to the left if he's on his way back to you). Try having somebody stand near the start/finish line and step in toward him as he's going by, to push him to the right or left. Also, if you're his handler, make sure you are well over to the left side of the runback area with his reward – really exaggerate it by standing near the start/finish line and way over to the left, and call him loudly.

Or you may have a swerver, who will often make a nice big arc instead of running straight up the lane to avoid another dog or handler. Swerving really slows down your dog's time and makes getting an accurate pass really difficult for you. Your dog could easily progress from swerving to running around the first jump altogether, too. To prevent swerving, put a gate on the right side of the lane so that the dogs have to run up the lane in a straight line. You can start out by putting the gate far away and tightening up with each session if you need to.

Racing Next to Another Dog

Once your dog is used to passing dogs in his own lane, it's time to race him against dogs in another lane. Hopefully you've already been doing side-by-side recalls next to other dogs. If you haven't, that's where you need to start, before you add the box into the equation.

Side by side recalls

Put an experienced confident dog in the other lane – use a dog that your dog can't break, basically (and that won't break your dog if your dog crosses over!).

Start with just one jump (the one by the start/finish line):

Have somebody hold your dog behind that jump in one lane and somebody else hold the other dog behind the first jump in the other lane. You and the other handler should be on the opposite side of the jumps.

Call your dog in a very excited happy way – wave your tug at him (or hold up your food) to draw his attention to you. The person holding him should let him go once it's clear that he's focused on you (and the holder in the other lane should sync up, too, so that they're letting the other dog go at approximately the same time).

Reward your dog when he comes to you.

If your dog comes over the jump to you and has good focus (he stays with you, or plays with his toy) both dogs and handlers should go ahead and move back a jump, until you have worked up to four jumps and you're ready to do full recalls. If your dog is looking hard at the other dog or crossing over, you may want to put up ring gates or fencing between the lanes, or get a line of people to stand there and block your dog from crossing over (if your dog does cross over, somebody needs to catch him quickly, in an unemotional matter-of-fact way, and carry or lead him back to you).

Once your dog is doing good focused recalls over four jumps next to another dog, take both dogs down to the box area and do some jump-box-jump drills (start out with just one jump). From there you can back up one jump at a time until you feel like you're ready to do full runs.

Full runs against another dog

Don't forget to switch lanes from time to time (it's probably best not to switch lanes right in the middle of a training session, though). You don't want your dog getting used to running in just one lane (this happens a lot, actually). Even though the lanes are set up in an identical way, the racing experience is different for your dog depending on which lane he's in – he's either going to see another dog next to him when he turns on the box or he's not, depending on which direction he turns and which lane he's in. This can really blow a dog's mind at first, if he's not used to it.

With all of this stuff you just have to trust your instincts and remind yourself not to push your dog too much. You don't want him to chase another dog and hurt it or get himself hurt, so be conservative. You have time to get this right. The last thing you want to do is walk into a tournament and have your dog chase another dog during competition – this is a surefire way to get your dog excused from the tournament and written up by the judge (or worse, get him banned from flyball).

Chasing

A dog that chases other dogs is one of my biggest pet peeves because it negatively affects other dogs and handlers. Chasers tend to stress out everybody – you never know what they might do to the dog they are chasing, or how that other dog might react to them. Even if the chasers mean no harm and are only "visiting" they're still a safety hazard because they're usually getting in the way somehow.

Chasing is self-rewarding, so you need to make other activities, like playing with you, even more rewarding.

In some ways, it's great that your dog is so interested in the other lane – it means he's aware of who he's racing against and whether or not they're beating him. Competitive dogs like this often make spectacular start dogs or anchor dogs. They will be the ones constantly glancing over to the other lane with that "Bring it!" look on their face, the ones who will try harder than anybody else to win.

There are lots of different ways to refocus a chaser. My Border Collie Kraken was a pretty bad herder (yes, he's the one who also didn't like balls), so the first thing we did was put a line of ring gating between the lanes in practice so he couldn't cross over. (You can also get people to stand there and hold the gates – it sort of looks like they're playing the accordion. This is a great way to keep dogs from crossing over because the human blocker can be detached and mechanical – the gate extends a person's arm reach by 10 feet so the person doesn't have to chase after or grab a dog that's getting ready to cross. They can just quickly step towards the dog and put up a gate barrier instead.)

I worked on small pieces of the game with Kraken (like close-up box work or recalls) while there was a dog running in the other lane. I made sure the dog in the other lane was pretty laid back, I didn't want Kraken working next to any amped-up speed demons yet.

The accordion gate method in action - this is at a workshop where two green dogs were practicing next to each other. We had a line of people between the two lanes holding gates in case either dog tried to cross over.

As his handler, I also worked really hard on being as exciting as I could be. Any time Kraken started to head over towards the other lane, I would call his name very excitedly, smack the tug on the floor to tease him, then run away from him a little bit, which usually was enough to pull his attention back over to me. I tugged with him a lot at home, too, to build up his tug drive.

After a while he was able to stay focused on me (or at least run right back to me when I called him), so we took the gates down and continued to desensitize him to motion and other dogs by the box and in the runback areas. I would stand about ten feet away from the box and play tug with Kraken while another dog raced. It's hard to do this with intensity for more than a couple of minutes – once your dog gets a little bored, his attention will shift right back over to the other dog. So we practiced this drill in short bursts. I would also stand in the runback area and play tug with Kraken while another dog was doing full runs.

Then we would switch places and let Kraken do full runs while another dog was tugging with somebody down near his box or in the runback area. He was very distracted at first (there were a lot of dropped balls!) and I had to work to stay upbeat and positive. I asked my teammates to step in whenever necessary to keep him away from another dog or to act like a human wall. It was my goal to always be the happy person with the tug that he wanted to come back to – I didn't want to be the one correcting him for anything.

When I went to tournaments I would also tug with Kraken on the sidelines while racing was going on. He really wanted to bark at the other dogs and lunge around on his leash, so initially it was a lot of work getting him to play with the tug – lots of ridiculous-looking happy-voiced hopping around on my part – and when he did tug he'd do it with a vengeance, almost like he was taking his frustration out on the tug. Eventually he became a crazy sidelines tugger and stopped paying attention to what was going on around him. That's when I knew he was ready to go into the ring.

Next we did tournament warm-ups. We started out with restrained recalls. Once Kraken was doing solid focused recalls, I brought him down to the box for jump-box-jump drills, then eventually full runs (this was over the course of several tournaments). He often looked around wildly at the other side but he would not cross over.

Eventually we felt comfortable enough letting him run in anchor position (last). I would hold him up until I could tell that he was focused on the ball/box and was going to run down there when I let him go. Finally we worked on tightening up his passes.

Kraken is not an aggressive chaser, he's just an extremely herdy Border Collie. If your dog is chasing other dogs in a scary way, you really need to work for a long time on correcting this behavior. Don't put other dogs at risk (no game is worth that). You may need to seek out help from an experienced behaviorist or trainer.

When you're working with a dog that has multiple issues, work on fixing one thing at a time, then build on each skill. Don't try to train or change too many behaviors at once.

Standing for Measuring

This skill is only necessary for height dogs that will be playing NAFA flyball. U-FLI's measuring technique just requires a judge to put a little metal instrument next to your dog's front leg and take a quick measure – if you can hold your dog still for ten seconds (you can even hold him in your arms), you're all set.

Indy, a 1 ½ year-old rat terrier, is calmly being measured with a wicket by a NAFA judge. Indy is a rescue dog who is owned by Kim Fuller of Millville, MA. They race with ARFF. *(Photo by Dave Strauss)*

NAFA's measuring system is more like what you'd experience at an agility or conformation competition. Your dog must stand still, with a balanced stance that essentially looks like a show stance while a judge lowers the arm of a wicket down on his withers. NAFA covers this stance in detail (and provides diagrams) in their rulebook. They also have a decent measuring video on their website (http://www.flyball.org/training_videos.html) that shows correct and incorrect stances and explains the measuring process in detail.

The judge may ask you to move your dog's feet around to get a proper stance, and he may have to raise and lower the wicket a few times until he's comfortable with the measurement, so you need to teach your dog to stay nice and calm and still while all this is going on. Typically, the calmer and more relaxed your dog is, the more accurate (and oftentimes lower) the measurement will be.

This is a lot to ask for some dogs. But you can train this pretty easily with a clicker and lots of treats.

I bought a cheap wicket online to practice with (just Google "dog wicket" to find them), but you can also practice by standing your dog next to a wall and laying a small level across his shoulders (I used to just use a pencil until a teammate pointed out to me that the pencil was always slanted one way or another). The level sort of simulates the feel of the wicket, too. Once you're sure your level is level, you can mark that area on the wall with a pencil and measure it with a tape measure later. Focus on teaching your dog to stand still at first. You can worry about his actual stance and foot placement later in the training process.

Sit down on the floor in front of your dog. Hold a treat out low in front of him (pinched between your fingers or tucked in your fist), and keep the treat just out of reach until he relaxes and stands still for a moment – then click and let him nibble on the treat while you're still holding it. Repeat this over and over until the dog understands that he only gets to sample the treat when he is standing still and waiting, not when he is lunging after it.

Once he is doing this reliably, start touching his feet and moving them into position. He may be very distracted by this at first and look wildly around to see what in the world you're doing to him. Just be very patient and reward him for every quiet stand.

When his stand looks good and you can move his feet around, start adding the level or wicket in to the mix. He'll adjust quickly to the pressure of the level or wicket on his back because he's already used to having you touch his feet and legs, and he knows that the treat is right there and he's going to get it soon.

You're allowed to use treats during the official measuring session with the judge, so if you train this right your dog should actually *enjoy* standing there getting easy treats during the measuring process.

Once your dog is standing well for you, ask other people to measure him. Start out with friends or family members, and then ask people the dog doesn't know.

You can also ask judges at tournaments to measure your dog for practice. Most judges are happy to do this. The wicket is usually only available on Saturday mornings (since measuring takes place about half an hour before the tournament starts), so you may want to ask the judge ahead of time if you can measure your dog right after the official measuring session is over.

"Out" (Drop it) Command

It's helpful to train your dog to spit out their ball or tug on command so that you can get them ready to line up and race again.

The way I teach this at home is to play tug with the dog, then gently take hold of his collar, let the toy go "dead" (by not playing with it anymore) and wait for him to drop the toy. Most dogs will drop it instinctively, but if your dog is a tougher case you can trade treats for the toy (and use a clicker to mark the behavior when he drops it). After your dog drops the toy, reward him by picking it back up and playing with him again a few times, so he gets used to the idea that dropping it doesn't mean that all the fun is going to end. In flyball, dropping it usually means he gets to run another heat!

You can also trade one tennis ball for another if your dog doesn't like to spit out his ball. I will play Chuckit with my dogs and have another ball waiting in the Chuckit queue to throw as soon as they drop the first one.

I have one dog (a Border Collie/Staffordshire Bull Terrier mix) who listens to "Out" just fine at home, but absolutely will not drop his tug in a tournament setting. He has very strong bully jaws, so to physically remove the tug you'd have to risk getting your fingers chomped or practically choke him off of the tug by holding his collar and one front leg (so he can't grab the tug with both front legs) until he dropped it. I've found a much better way to do it now. I hold him around his waist by his hips and pick him up, dangling him upside down until he drops the tug, which usually takes less than 10 seconds and causes him no discomfort (it looks funny, though!).

Running for a Different Handler

Once your dog has been racing for a while, it's smart to have him practice racing for somebody else (a teammate, friend, or spouse) so that if you ever get another dog, hurt yourself and can't run, or get sick the day before the tournament, your dog will happily run for somebody else.

Handling – Skills for People

General Attitude

The most important thing you can bring to flyball training is a positive attitude and a sense of humor. Never forget that this is a game that's supposed be fun for you and your dog. Ideally your dog will race because he loves it and he wants to, not just because you tell him to.

As if having fun isn't a good enough motivation all on its own, it also inspires your dog's best performance. The fastest dogs are the ones who can't wait to play, who love it so much that they'll run as fast as they can every time, no matter what distractions are around them or how tired they are.

I see so many people out there in the lanes who don't really play with their dog – they just stand there and talk with teammates or watch the race while their dog dances around trying to engage them. Play with your dog! They'll run better for you!

Lane Choreography

When you first start playing flyball it's going to feel a little bit like your first day in step aerobics class. Everybody else will be moving around so effortlessly while you're tripping over your own feet trying to keep up. Don't worry, it gets easier!

There's a specific traffic pattern that everybody follows during a race:

- At the beginning of each heat, the start dog handler lines his dog up in the center of the racing lane and waits for the light tree to start its countdown. Everybody else lines up on the right-hand side of the racing lane and waits for their turn to run.

- When the start-dog handler lets his dog go, he runs up the center of the lane for several feet, and then steps over to the left side of the lane so that the next handler will have a clear view to release his dog. This part is easy for the start dog handler because he's the first one in the lane, but subsequent handlers will need to wait until the dog in front of them passes by before they can step over to the left, or somebody's gonna get run over.

This is Fur Fun at the 2012 NAFA CanAm Classic tournament. The start dog, Elphaba (not visible), is on her way back and her handler, Leerie Jenkins, is heading into the runback area holding the tug in his left hand. Julie Norman Jenkins has just released Rip, the blue merle Border Collie. Waiting to go next is Rose Lynch with Joy (Rip's sister), and Ben Hill and Hotblack are in anchor position. Scott Chamberlain is judging. (Sidenote: Usually there's not a huge crowd of people standing behind you watching your every move during racing - this photo was taken on the final day of the biggest tournament in flyball, during one of the championship division races.)
(Photo by Dave Strauss)

- Most handlers will continue to run toward the start/finish line until their dog turns on the box and sees them – then they'll turn and run in the opposite direction toward the runback area, holding their tug in their left hand to make it easy for the dog to grab (plus this ensures that the dog will run straight up the lane versus swerving crazily to the right side after the tug).

- The anchor-dog handler (whose dog runs last, hence the term **"anchor"**) should still get in the habit of moving over to the left, even though there are usually no dogs behind him in the lineup, because you never know when there might be a flag and a dog will have to re-run.

- At the end of the heat, everybody plays with their dog in the run-back area until it's time to line up for the next heat.

- When the race is over, everybody tells the other team "Good race" and shakes hands if possible (sometimes this is hard to do if you're hustling to clip your leash on your excited dog), then both teams move out of the ring as soon as possible so the next teams can bring their dogs in.

Handling a Dog in Start Position

When you see two revved-up start dogs tensely waiting for the lights on the light tree to count down, it's easy to see why flyball is sometimes called "Drag racing for dogs." Ready…Set…*GO!*

Before each heat begins, the judge will ask each start-dog handler if they are ready to go. He'll probably do it by making eye contact with you, holding his hand up in your direction, and waiting for you to nod or say "Yes." Before you nod, give a quick look around to make sure the rest of your teammates are ready to go (including your box loader – and make sure there's a ball in the box!). Be clear with your nod – make it distinct. Once both of the start-dog handlers nod, the judge will start the race and the countdown on the light tree will begin.

The lights will quickly run up to the top of the light tree, then flash in one-second intervals on the way down (U-FLI's start light cadence interval is 1.2 seconds, and while NAFA's are set to the 1.0 second cadence).

Most handlers let their dog go on the second yellow light. At the green light they say "Ready," at the first yellow light they say "Set," and at the second yellow light they say "Go" as they release the dog.

🐕 *This is Sure Shots all lined up and ready to go. Sonya Barton is handling the start dog, Impulse, and watching the judge. Other team members from L to R: Steve Hudson with Shay (a rescued mixed breed), Cindy Dalton with Myles Moy, and Robbie Barton with Sly Moy. (**Photo by Len Silvester**)*

Where to start your dog depends on the dog's speed – a 4.0 dog is generally released from 43-45 feet (on the second yellow light) in NAFA racing and 53-55 feet in U-FLI racing.

As soon as your dog crosses the start line, you'll be able to see the start time on the digital display. If it was a false start, the red light at the top of the light tree will flash, the digital display will show a negative number, and the judge will blow the whistle. Otherwise you'll see a time up on the display that lets you know how close you were to nailing it. The closer you get to .000, the better (and a handler who consistently gets a .0-something start is considered to be very good).

Each team is allowed one false start per heat, except in NAFA's Veterans division (the idea being that older dogs shouldn't be worn out with a bunch of false starts). Most false starts occur because the handlers are pushing for perfection and just happen to let go a little early, or because the dog is especially fired up. You'll run into the occasional competitor

🐕 *Awesome .001 start by Meg Shipley and Border Whippet Dose (not visible) of Rocket Relay. Following Dose is Habit, the team's mixed-breed height dog owned by Don Blewett. Third is Method, a Border Collie handled by Kelly Robbins-Walt, and in anchor is Vixen, a Belgian Malinois handled by Aaron Robbins. This photo was taken on Day 3 of the 2012 NAFA CanAm Classic. **(Photo by Dave Strauss)***

who false starts on purpose, either to gain a competitive edge by psyching you out or tiring out your dog, or because they have a very green dog and want to give him one more "practice run" before the actual race begins. The intentional false starts are rare but they do happen.

If a handler gets two false starts in the same heat, it's considered an error (just like an early pass would be) and their dog is required to re-run at the end to complete the heat.

Passing

Good passing benefits every team, no matter what division you're in. Tight passes can shave a full second or two off your team's total time, which comes in handy whether you're trying to break records or earn the maximum number of points each heat.

It always baffles me when people/clubs focus on how to make their dogs faster but don't work on their own passing skills. On a four-second dog, each foot of passing equals about .033 seconds. So a three-foot pass on a four-second dog adds approximately one-tenth of a second to their time (so a 4.0 dog is now 4.1). And a three-foot pass actually isn't bad! Most yucky passes are more in the ten-foot-plus range.

The Formula

Passing freaks a lot of people out at first, especially if the dogs involved are particularly fast, but the passing formula is actually pretty simple.

First, you identify a **passing window** – a mental snapshot of what you want to see the dog in front of you doing when you let your dog go. Some people like to let their dog go when the dog in front of them is turning on the box. Others like to wait until the dog is clearing the first hurdle after the box (sometimes called the "5th jump") on the way back. It's all up to

This is my favorite passing window - the dog has turned completely on the box and is centered back over the lane, ball in mouth. When I'm passing a dog with an inconsistent turn (or one that tends to bobble balls) I'll wait until the first jump to let my dog go instead. **(Photo by Len Silvester)**

you – use whatever cue you want, as long as you can anticipate it and see it consistently. Sometimes it helps to videotape the dog in front of you during practice then watch the video in slow motion so you can really get familiar with the way the dog turns on the box and takes the jumps.

Next you're going to adjust where you stand based on how close your passes are. Don't change your passing window/mental snapshot, only change where you are standing.

The only exception to this rule is if the dog in front of you does something funny, like bobbles their ball as they're catching it, stutter-steps in between jumps, or turns exceptionally wide off the box. In that case you need to hold your dog slightly longer than you normally would to prevent an early pass or collision, because that dog is going to be slower coming back.

Where to start your dog

At almost every tournament there is a measuring tape attached to the floor in each lane so that you know exactly where to stand with your dog. If you have no idea where to stand at first, ask your teammates or other competitors for some help – they'll probably ask you how fast your dog is and how fast the dog in front of you is, and from there they can provide a basic guesstimate. Start out conservatively at first – if your pass is huge, you can move up a little after each heat once you get some feedback about how big it actually is.

Although every handler loves to get such a perfect pass that the line judge and pass-caller flinch and look up at the light tree (which would flash a red light to indicate the pass was early), it's not best practice to try for the heart-attack pass every time. If you have an early pass, your team could lose the heat and possibly also miss out on the points, if you can't re-run your dog fast enough. A one-foot or two-foot pass is really great, and you take some pressure off yourself if you aim for a two-foot pass instead of a perfect pass.

If your pass caller tells you that you have a three-foot pass, only move up one foot to close the distance. It would be nice if the formula was as simple as "You had a three-foot pass so move up three feet to close the distance," but it doesn't work that way (due to human reaction time and also because the dogs are closing the distance between each other at varying speeds). In fact, if somebody tells me I have a five-foot pass, I'll still just move up one foot at a time until I get it right.

🐕 *This is Rude Dogs, lining up with precision and working together like a well-oiled machine. Left to right is Coach John Skalski with Octane going by, Sasha Falk handling Edge (not visible), Sharron Nevens handling Amp, and Bill Pinder handling Diesel. Bill owns Diesel and the other dogs are owned by Connie Croley Skalski.* **(Photo by Len Silvester)**

Years ago, flyball competitors lined their dogs up around the 20-foot line to pass until they discovered that their dogs ran faster if they backed them up (because more distance gave the dogs more time/running surface to work up to full speed). A rough calculation, based on a 4.0 second dog, is that a dog will run about one tenth of a second faster for every 10 feet you move back (this is especially true for bigger dogs – smaller dogs like terriers don't need as much room to work up to full speed). So if your dog runs a 4.2 from 20 feet, he'll run around 4.1 from 30 feet and 4.0 from 40 feet.

Since farther back generally equals faster, competitive handlers prefer to let their dogs go when the dog in front of them is turning on the box. You can't release any sooner than that because it would be a terrible safety hazard to do so – you need to wait until the dog in front of you has caught his ball and has committed himself to running back (e.g., he's not chasing a bobbled ball).

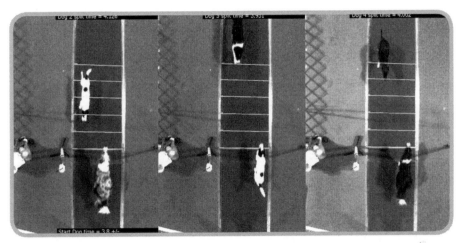

Overhead view of dogs passing during one heat of racing, taken by Dave Thomas' amazing Automated Pass Evaluation System (APES). First pass is about 2 feet, second pass is about 5 feet, third pass is about 4 feet. **(Photo by Dave Thomas)**

If the dog in front of you is out of shape or older and slows down after a few heats, try standing in the same place for the first two heats, then back up a foot or two after every heat. That should prevent an early pass.

Since I'm usually running multiple dogs during a flyball weekend, I record where I'm standing for each pass on my phone to keep track (I have also written it on my arm in Sharpie pen!).

Calling passes

It's important to find a good pass caller to help you during races. It can be somebody on your team who's not in that race, somebody from another team, or even a friend or spouse who's not competing but has a good eye. Pass callers usually stand at the start/finish line on the outside of the ring, right behind the line judge.

Most tournaments have the first 5-6 feet of the lane marked with duct tape in one-foot increments on the mat to help pass callers out.

Here is the magic tip: pass callers should look to see where the second dog is when the first dog's nose crosses the start/finish line, *not* for where the two dogs' noses cross each other.

For example, if Dog #1's nose is crossing the start/finish line when Dog #2's nose is at the three-foot line, the pass is three feet. The dogs will actually cross each other somewhere around 1-2 feet, but the pass is still three feet.

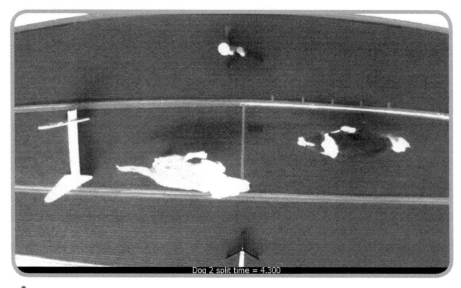

Dog 2 split time = 4.300

In this shot taken from directly over the start/finish line, you can clearly see this 2-foot pass. (Photo by Dave Thomas, Automated Pass Evaluation System (APES))

You can also videotape the passes with a digital camera or smartphone that has a slow-motion playback feature. Just film the actual *passes* – begin the video right before the start dog and second dog pass each other, and end it right after the third and fourth dogs pass each other. This gives you time to quickly rewind the video and play it back, watch the passes, and notify the team so they can adjust accordingly. At first it might be a little overwhelming trying to play back the video that quickly (there's not much time between heats), but you'll get better at it with practice. In the meantime you can all review the passes at the crating area after the race is over and make adjustments to your passes in the next race.

How to hold your dog during the race

There are a lot of different ways to hold your dog when you're getting ready to release him. The most important thing is to be consistent in the way you hold him and to pay attention to where you are next to the measuring tape before each heat.

Hard Drive's "A" team, Kilabite: Kris Patzer is handling Dan Nerl's Border Collie, Stetson, in start. Howie Zeamer is next to them with Cyber, his very enthusiastic Border Staffy. Kim Zeamer is holding Remix (not visible) and Andy Patzer is holding Mesa (not visible). (Photo by Marsha Lundy-Almond)

Some handlers like to sit on their knees and pull their dogs up against the front of their thighs or into their laps to give them a good launching pad. Others bend one knee and pull their dog against them but keep the dog's back feet on the floor, while others crouch over their dog or stand next to him and hold his collar or harness. Do whatever works best for you and your dog.

When you line up, make sure you follow the same routine every time. I like to use my dog's front feet as my guide – for instance, I might line my dog up so that his front toes are always at the 50-foot line.

🐕 *Pam Casselman of Burnin' Rubber holds her Whippet, Reach, and counts down the start.* **(Photo by Len Silvester)**

Please don't "bowl" your dog down the lane! **Bowling** is when a handler uses the dog's collar or harness to propel him into the lane when it's his turn to run. You'll totally throw him off balance when you do that (plus it looks mean). It's sort of like shoving your kid in the pool right before he's getting ready to dive in himself. If your dog won't run down to the box unless you bowl him, you have some work to do back at practice. Technically, a judge can flag you for "inappropriately assisting" your dog if you bowl him.

Sportsmanship

Flyball is a sport where everybody steps up to help each other, regardless of what club they're in. Small clubs or short-handed clubs will often help each other at tournaments – they might box load for each other's races, shag balls, or even handle dogs for each other.

Club lines have blurred even more in recent years with NAFA's introduction of Open and Veterans classes and U-FLI's Pickup teams. It used to be that you could only run your dog with your own club, but with Open,

Veterans and Pickup, you can now build teams of dogs from many different clubs. This has led to a lot more camaraderie at tournaments (it's hard to be aloof toward your rivals when you're racing with them on an Open team).

Here are some general etiquette guidelines to follow:

- Be pleasant out in the lanes when you're racing.

- Shake hands or say "Good race" when the race is over (whether you win or lose).

- Be respectful toward the judge, even if you disagree with his call – it's okay to approach him and ask for clarification around a call, but it's not okay to get in his face and argue with him.

- If your dog does something silly during a race, like crosses over into the other lane to chase a bobbled ball, apologize to the other team.

- Help other people out, whether they're in your club or not – hold the door for them if they're struggling with a big crate, offer them a baggie if their dog is pooping and they are blustering around through their pockets looking for a bag, volunteer to sit in the line-judging and box-judging chairs if you have a break for a few races.

- Watch your language during racing – a lot of spectators on the sidelines are kids.

Also, cut your teammates some slack if they make a mistake. If they have a bad pass, or a double false start, or get in your way so that you can't see to let your dog go, don't yell at them. It's easy to get frustrated, especially in the heat of the moment during a race, but you'll be glad you held your tongue when you're the one making a mistake and everybody else gives you a break. It's all part of being on a team.

Be an Asset, Not a Liability

You and/or your dog can always improve somewhere. Don't get complacent. You or your dog handicaps the team if:

- Your dog is inconsistent – he drops his ball or runs around the jumps a lot, or his box turn is so unpredictable that everybody has a hard time passing into him.

- Your dog is out of shape and tires easily (making him harder to pass and making your team slower).

- You're not a very good passer – your passes are either so big that they add significantly to your team's total time, or you have so many early passes that your team's total time (after your dog's re-run) is too slow to earn points.

- You don't understand the rules – this can cost your team the race if you re-run your dog out of order or something like that.

- You're not a very good starter – your starts are so big that they add significantly to your team's total time, or you double false start a lot, requiring your dog to re-run (which may take you out of points contention that heat).

- You don't know how to call passes – sometimes you may be the only person available (not running a dog or box loading) to call passes for one of your teams, and if you don't know how, your team's performance will suffer for it.

- Your dog can only run in start or anchor – this restricts what the rest of the team can do.

These are all things you have control over. You can fix these things!

Strategy – Skills for Teams

Determining Lineups and Seed Times

Lineups

Sometimes your lineups determine themselves if you have a lot of dogs who can only run in certain positions or pass into certain dogs.

Examples of this would be the dog that can only run in anchor because he drops his ball or runs around the jump if the dog passing into him is too close, or a handler who is only able to run his dog in start position because he's terrible at passing.

If you can get these issues fixed, you'll have a lot more options when it comes to lineups.

Here's a good recipe for putting dogs together:

- The *start dog* should be competitive (loves racing against the dog in the other lane) and very physically fit because if there are a lot of false starts he could end up running twice as much as the rest of the dogs on the team. He needs to be really focused down on the box/ball – the type of dog who will not get confused about which lane he's supposed to be in. It's best not to put your height dog in start position because they have to jump proportionately higher than the other dogs on the team (especially in NAFA) and will wear out faster with false starts.

- The *second and third dogs* should run as fast in the pack as they would in start or anchor. Their handlers need to be good passers and the dogs should be able to take a really tight pass from either direction.

- The *anchor dog* should be competitive. You know the type – they turn on the afterburners to beat the dog next to them. A lot of teams like to put their fastest dog in anchor. In addition to being a good passer, the anchor dog's handler should be able to assess what's going on in the other lane during the race (whether or not that team is ahead, or if they have a flag) and act accordingly.

The more consistent you are with your lineups, the faster your teams' times will be. The dogs and handlers get used to passing each other in a certain order, and develop confidence and a rhythm. You could mess up your time by half a second or more just by mixing up the same four dogs and handlers into a different running order (at least until they got used to running in the new order, which could take several tournaments).

Seed times

To estimate a seed time for a team of four dogs, you can either take their average times and add them together, or take each of their best times and add a second to that total to account for passing (my old club captain actually added 0.8 of a second instead, which was a good formula based on the way our team passed).

To get average times for all the dogs in your club, keep track of their performance for a few tournaments. Some teams appoint a statistician to write down the dogs' split times every single heat of every single race, then input it all into a spreadsheet and generate a post-tournament report highlighting each dog's performance. You can record the data (start times, split times, total team times) off the digital displays behind the boxes.

It used to be that the only way you knew what your dog's times were was for somebody to write them down for you and show you after the race. These days, with the digital displays, you can see what your dog ran every heat if you want to (if you remember to look up at the digital display fast enough!). If you've been racing your dog for a while, and your passing is pretty consistent, you'll have a pretty good idea of your dog's average time just based on what you've seen on the digital displays.

If you decide to seed your team based on each dog's best time, be sure to add in around one second's worth of padding for starts and passing since most dogs' best times are recorded when their starts or passes are near-perfect.

Like this:

Dog	Best time
Start dog	4.1
Dog #2	4.2
Dog #3	4.8
Anchor dog	4.0
Sub-Total	**17.1**
Padding	1.0
Total Seed Time	**18.1**

It's important to seed your team as accurately as possible because that's how the tournament director is going to decide which racing division to put your team in.

There's also a "break-out time" for every division (except Division 1) to discourage sandbagging (**sandbagging** is when a team intentionally seeds itself slower than it should so it can stomp everybody in its division). The **break-out time** is one second faster than the seed time for the fastest team in that division (so if the fastest team in Division 2 is seeded at 17.1 seconds, the break-out time would be 16.1 seconds). If your team breaks out, you automatically lose the heat, and after three break-outs your team is ineligible for tournament placement (you can still race and earn title points, though).

Division 1, whether it's in Regular, Multibreed/Variety, or Open class, doesn't have a break-out time because the goal in Division 1 is to run the fastest time you can.

Green Dogs

Green dogs (what we call the young dogs or newbies) are the future of your team! Take the time to work with them in warm-ups and make their introduction to competition positive and fun.

Warm-up slots

If you have green dogs, try to arrange it so that they're on a team where they get to use most of the warm-up time. Green dogs are sometimes overwhelmed by the noise and motion at a tournament, so start out by doing easy drills like restrained recalls and close-up box work, then work up to full runs over the course of the weekend (some green dogs spend a whole tournament just doing recalls in warm-ups, and that's okay!).

Get the whole team involved in warm-ups when a green dog is out there. You will probably need additional props, runners/clappers, and maybe even a line of people to stand between the lanes in case the green dog gets a little goofy and decides to run into the other side's lane or runback area.

If my club has a green dog that does really great in warm-ups – a perfect full run while focused on their handler – we try to harness this positive momentum and put him into an actual race as soon as possible.

One of my favorite parts about flyball is watching the light bulb come on over a green dog's head in a tournament. With some dogs you really can see it happen – it's like they're saying "OHHHHH, *this* is why we've been doing all that stuff in practice for the past few months!"

In the lineup

It's a good idea to run green dogs in start position or anchor position for a few tournaments, because both of these positions have unique advantages (see below) and also only require the dog to take one pass. Have the green dog pass into a dog that won't intimidate him (this could be the height dog or a mild-mannered bigger dog).

Also, keep the pressure off the green dog/handler team as much as possible by putting them on a "fun" team versus a more competitive one (if your club has teams in several divisions). Green dogs often make mistakes and/or require bigger passes at first, so the team they're on might not get as many points or win as many heats as a team with more experienced dogs on it. Set the green dogs and their handlers up to succeed. Go into it with the mindset that it's okay to lose races or not get so many points now because you're hoping that the green dog will benefit your team later.

You can have a green dog share a spot with a solid backup, too – this gives you the option to pull them out of the lineup if they fall apart or do something goofy. Don't let them keep making the same mistake over and over again – use your warm-ups in the next race to try to fix the problem.

Start position

If the green dog loves to race other dogs and is really focused down on the ball/box, put him in start position. It will build up his confidence because as the start dog he can run full-speed into an open, empty lane, and the start routine of "Ready…Set…*GO*" with the light countdown is predictable but very exciting.

Have the handler of the second dog take it easy on the pass – start out with a big pass and scoot up a tiny bit (6 inches or a foot) every heat as long as the green dog seems okay with it.

Anchor position

If the green dog gets distracted by the other lane, or forgets which lane he's supposed to be in sometimes, or gets more revved up by the other dogs barking around him, put him in anchor position.

Anchor position is also good for dogs and handlers who haven't mastered the lane choreography yet – if they're the last to run, they're less likely to get in anybody else's way (although they do need to know what to do if one of the first three dogs has to re-run after the anchor dog).

Warm-ups

Each team gets a one- or two-minute warm-up period before every race (often a tournament will start out with a two-minute warm-up period and then switch to a one-minute warm-up at a pre-determined point in the race schedule to save time). Only the dogs listed on the timesheet for that team can participate in the warm-up, and dogs must be at least a year old to be listed on a timesheet.

Most judges start the warm-up countdown as soon as the previous race is over and those teams have removed their boxes from the ring. That means if you want to get anything out of your warm-up time at all, you should be waiting with your dog next to the ring or right outside the door (if your dog is a crazy barker).

You can pack a lot into one or two minutes, especially if your team is organized and everybody knows what their job is ahead of time. You can stage timed one- or two-minute warm-ups in your practices to prepare for the tournament situation.

Restrained recalls are a great way to get the dogs pumped up and let them know which lane they're racing in. During tournaments it really helps to have somebody other than the box loader waiting down in the box area to hold dogs and release them for recalls. The box loader will be busy getting the box and props and balls in, which eats up valuable warm-up time.

🐕 *Dog being held for a restrained recall during a tournament warm-up period.*
(Photo by Willie Moore)

Some dogs benefit from working on their box turns close up, as you did when you were beginning to train. Use a prop in front of the box during warm-ups. You can also run dogs the full length of the course with the prop in front of the box.

Warm-ups are also a good time to practice your passing. You can get in one or two full runs (even after restrained recalls) and get feedback about your passes from a pass caller so that you know where to stand during the race. Just be careful not to run your dog too much – you don't want to wear him out before the race even begins.

Make judicious use of props during warm-ups. At the very least, always put a prop in front of the box if you're doing any box work. Some teams bring in gates to work on dogs who like to skirt the jumps, or put pieces of plastic gutter or wooden slats on the floor to remind the dog of where to approach or land off the box.

Teams are also expected to set their jump heights during the warm-up period, so it's handy to have someone who is designated to do that.

When the judge blows the whistle, the warm-up period is over and all practice must stop. You should immediately stop whatever you're doing and go to the runback area to line up your dog. Judges get irritated if you let your dog go for a practice run after they've blown the whistle (technically, they could flag you for "training in the ring" and you'd lose the first heat), or if you delay the start of the race by more than a few seconds (by putting away green dogs, setting up jumps, etc.).

Organizing Practices and Classes

Flyball Practices

You'll see a lot of quick progress if your club is able to get together weekly for practice. Your dog will benefit from regular sessions on the flyball box (especially if you don't have one at home to practice on) and from working around other dogs and people. Regular practices also motivate you to train more at home – it keeps flyball in the front of your brain.

Places to practice

Finding somewhere to practice is often a challenge since flyball requires a lot of space – the flyball course is 51 feet and the runback area is another 50-60 feet or so.

Here are some places I've practiced before:

- **Teammate's yard.** This option works well if everybody lives fairly close to each other. It's free, there's usually a place to store all the equipment, there's a bathroom, and you can get together any day or time that you want. The downside is you're at the mercy of the weather, and the neighbors might get irritated with all the frantic barking.

- **Local kennel club.** Most cities have a kennel club where dog events like obedience or conformation shows are held. They are usually large, with a concrete floor. Renting one on a weekly basis can be expensive, though, and you have to fit your practice into the kennel club's schedule. They may or may not have somewhere you can store your equipment, and you'll definitely need mats to run on concrete.

- **Dog Day Cares or Training Facilities.** These are usually smaller than kennel clubs, so you probably won't have room to set up a full lane plus runback area, but you could at least do recalls and box work with one or two jumps instead of four. Dog day cares and training facilities often have matting on the floor already (although some of the rough or pebbled matting will still burn the dogs' pads if they're running fast on it). I found several local dog day cares who were willing to let me practice there for free in exchange for publicity (I held a flyball class there, which brought potential clients to their buildings). But it really just depends on the business. You also have to work your practice into their schedule and follow their rules.

- **Local park.** If you go this route, make sure it's okay for you to be there, you don't want to the Parks & Rec people to show up and kick you out. Flyball practices can be loud. Parks usually have nice long flat stretches of grass, they're free, and you have some flexibility with days/times. The downside of practicing in public like this is that you'll probably get a lot of people walking up (some with their dogs) asking what you're doing and even wanting to participate.

- **Parking decks.** I know of several ingenious clubs who practice in corporate parking decks on weekends when the businesses are closed. You will need to bring your own mats to practice on concrete (which will require a truck or even a small trailer), but parking decks have nice big flat stretches of concrete *and* there are levels that are shaded and covered from the rain! Plus you don't have to worry about finding a place to park.

- **Barns.** When I was on a team in New England, we practiced in a big horse barn. Not my favorite place to practice, because the floor was a sand/dirt mix (which meant dirty dogs and clogged flyball boxes) and it was *cold* in that barn in January, but it was definitely big enough.

Get creative about where you can practice in your area. Other ideas: indoor sports complexes (soccer arenas), recreation centers, fairgrounds,

🐾 *Practicing outside in a teammate's yard.*

hockey rinks (for my Canadian friends), warehouses, or convention centers. There is a great tournament held twice a year in Talladega, AL, at a Baptist convention center (in their recreation hall, which is a huge air-conditioned gym with a wood floor). You just never know where you'll hit on the perfect place.

Practice agenda

It helps to have a practice plan/format that everyone is aware of beforehand. Otherwise practice can drag on and on, or disintegrate into a lot of little groups talking and playing with their dogs without much getting done.

Here are some good ground rules to follow:

❶ Allow dogs to socialize with each other before and after practice (while you're setting up or breaking down the equipment, for example), but during practice ask everyone to put their dog away and focus on one dog (or pair of dogs, or team of dogs) at a time.

❷ Write down the names of all the dogs on a piece of paper or a whiteboard at the beginning of practice, and work with them in that order. That way everybody knows when their dog is "on deck" and can go get them pottied and ready while the dog before them is working.

❸ Keep each dog's session short (around 10 minutes).

❹ Require everybody to participate in each drill, even when it's not their dog out there. They can load the box, shag balls, run next to the dog, or videotape. (An exception to this would be if a handler wants to bring their dog out on a leash near the lane and do some focus work – this is a great use of time if there are already enough people available to help with the drill.)

Most clubs like to practice for a few hours every weekend or on a weeknight after work. Others get together less often due to location/distance/weather (if you practice outside and you live somewhere that's cold in January, you might take a winter hiatus, for example), so team members may try to work with their dogs by themselves at home in between practices. Some ambitious clubs have a big organized practice one day a week and a smaller weekly practice at somebody's house (e.g., garage, basement) just to do close-up box work.

Drills

Below are some drills you can do during practice. Every dog is different, so mix and match based on the individual dog's needs.

Box drills

Always use a prop in front of the box for these drills! Average placement for the jump board is around one foot away from the front of the box.

Hit-its on and off the box (without the ball):

- This drill is for dogs who are just starting out on the box (with no ball added yet). Lure the dog quickly on and off the box with food, a tug, or a target (for more details, read the box training chapter). Once his turn looks good and it's clear that he understands what he's supposed to do, assign a command like "Hit it" and fade out the lure (this will probably take several sessions/practices).

- Your goal is to be able to say "Hit it" (and point at the box, if necessary, but without the food/toy in your hand) and run in the opposite direction while your dog is doing his turn. When the dog catches you, reward him with a really yummy treat or fun game of tug. This will encourage him to snap off the box and execute a nice speedy turn.

- Whatever you do, *do not* have the box loader reward your dog with a treat for coming to the box, otherwise you're going to end up with a dog that stops on the box and looks up at the box loader expectantly.

Hit-its with a ball added:

- Once the dog is doing nice hit-its off the box, it's time to add a ball to the equation. Remember that often the turn falls apart at first as the dog readjusts his body (and his focus) to catch the ball. Tell the dog to get his ball, then run in the opposite direction and reward him when he completes his turn, catches the ball, and runs back to you.

- There may be several sub-steps to this drill, depending on the dog. If the dog has trouble catching the ball, for instance, you may have to stick the ball to the box with Velcro, or switch to a squishy foam ball instead of a regular tennis ball, or slow down the trigger speed on the box so it launches slower.

- If the dog has no interest in the ball, you may have to take the dog aside and play ball with him first to get him focused on it.

Box work with props:

- Once a dog is catching the ball out of the box, you can work more on his precision and speed. Watch carefully where he puts his feet on the box (ideally, videotape him and watch it in slow motion playback). If anything looks funky, use props around the box to direct how he is approaching it and where his feet land on it.

- Start out doing a lot of close-up box work, first without any jumps at all (letting him go from about 10-15 feet back), then from a few feet behind the first jump. Once you are happy with his turn and one jump, keep adding jumps until you work up to a full run. Continue to back him up and monitor his turn – sometimes when dogs speed up they have a harder time controlling their body so they start doing crazy things like sliding or crashing into the box.

- As he progresses, you can add elements to the drill that will make him faster, such as you calling his name a few steps before he hits the box, running away from him faster while showing him his reward, getting another person to stand down at the box and run next to him when he turns, or racing him against another dog.

Jumping drills

Restrained recalls

Recalls are a great drill for every dog, no matter how experienced they. The goal is for somebody to hold the dog at the box – it's great if that person can sit on top of the box and pull the dog back so that he can use the box pedal as a launching pad – while the handler is down in the runback area calling the dog and running in the opposite direction.

Power jumping

Increase the number of hurdles (set 10' apart) for a power jumping exercise to build up endurance. This drill works the same as the restrained recall, just with more jumps (5-7 instead of four).

Chase recalls

To speed up a dog you can have him do a recall behind another dog (one or two jump-lengths apart). If you do this, make sure that dog #2 is not the type who will blow off his handler and chase after dog #1 in the runback area. This drill is great for building speed and focus.

Side-by-side recalls

This is a great way to get green dogs used to running against another dog, or to speed up dogs who are motivated by competition.

Lineups

I was part of a club once where all we did was come to practice and run four-dog lineups. It got really boring – even the dogs were bored! It's best

The Beginner's Guide to Flyball

to just stick to five or so runs per team – lineups probably benefit the handlers more than the dogs (it's our way of working on our lane choreography and passing).

Passing drills

Introduction to passing

See Chapter 5 for details on how to introduce a green dog to passing.

Passing with multiple dogs

You can bring out two or more experienced dogs together and work on passing by having them line up in the runback area like they would in competition and do full runs. This is a good basic drill if the dogs are accustomed to passing in general, but the dog/handler needs to get used to passing a new dog before a tournament.

Have somebody stand at the start/finish line and call passes (and/or videotape). The handlers can adjust their distance based on this feedback. This is also a good time to put somebody in a chair where the line judge sits and the box judge sits to simulate a tournament environment (some dogs are really startled by box judges if they've never seen one before a tournament). These "judges" should wave a flag every now and then, too, but they should not interact with your dog while they're pretending to be a box judge.

Socialization & Distractions

Socialization is also really important, so you should also build time for that into your practices. I prefer to let the dogs socialize with each other (off lead, playing around) either before practice or after practice. It drives me nuts to have dogs barking on leashes or running around after a ball or whatever in the practice area when I'm trying to work with a green dog.

It is important, however, to get the dogs used to working around noise and chaos and distraction – it's not going to be a sterile quiet environment in a tournament, that's for sure. If you have enough people, set up two lanes and do as much work as you can in both lanes at the same time in a controlled organized way (some green dogs will be too distracted to have dogs working right next to them at first, but gradually get them used to it).

Try to make the transition from practice to a tournament as easy as possible by introducing the dogs to as many different variables and possible scenarios that you can think of ahead of time.

Flyball Classes

Offering flyball classes is a great way to recruit new team members and put a little money in your bank account to pay for equipment or tournament fees.

If you have enough interest in the class (5-10 prospective students), you can make it a six- or eight-week gig and meet weekly for an hour or so. If instead you seem to get one new person interested in class every 3-4 weeks, you may want to offer an ongoing "drop-in" type of class at a set time every week, where one instructor works with the more advanced dogs while another instructor tutors the newbies for a few sessions to bring them up to speed.

Young puppies shouldn't be in the regular flyball class because of the stress the jumping and box work puts on their joints (most puppies' growth plates don't close until they are 8-12 months old, depending on breed and structure). You could offer a puppy curriculum, however, where you work on focus, drive, or targeting until they're old enough for the other stuff.

Be sure to set expectations for the class participants up front. Dogs progress in their flyball training at different rates (depending on genetics, prior training, and how much homework the owner is willing to do in between classes), so not all of them are going to be able to complete a full run of the flyball course by the end of a six- or eight-week class. You may even want to break your class up into Beginner and Intermediate classes.

If your club has several people knowledgeable enough to teach the class, you can pack a lot more into the hour by splitting the class up into two groups and working half of the dogs on the box and the other half on the jumps or ball.

Here's a sample class agenda:

Beginner Class

Introduction to the game of flyball

Explain the rules and use some of your club's dogs to demonstrate how the game is played. Stress the importance of being a positive trainer (you may want to briefly cover clicker training or verbal marking). Explain rewards and how to create a motivational toy for your dog.

Recalls

Start with one jump. The instructor holds the dog a couple of feet behind the jump while the owner steps over the jump then turns around and lures dog over with food or toy. Add one jump at a time to the drill until dog is able to do recalls over all four jumps (use gating if necessary to prevent dogs from going around the jumps).

Ball retrieval

Roll the ball 5-10 times for the dog (holding him until ball is 10-15 feet away) to see which way he's going to turn. You'll need this info for box training, plus it lets you see whether the dog is interested in the ball or not.

Box work

If your club has a ramp, use that at first instead of a flyball box, because the ramp has more turning surface and a gentler angle. For flyball classes I prefer to train the box using Method #3 (over prop to box method) described in the Box Turn chapter. Some dogs are going to pop on and off the ramp/box on the first lesson, while others are going to take a while. You may have to show the owner how to lure the dog around his body onto the ramp at first if the dog won't leap on his own.

Socialization

Pay attention to how each dog interacts with the other dogs and with the instructors. If they have any issues (lack of focus, aggression), have a chat with the owner about how they can work on this at home. If necessary, recommend that they find an experienced behaviorist or trainer to help them with aggression-related issues.

It's fun to end each class with a group recall session – the students (dogs and human) love them. Have the students stand in a line down at the box and run one dog in a restrained recall at a time. As soon as a dog finishes his recall and is with his owner (and it's clear that his owner is in control of the situation) let the next dog go. After each recall have the handler bring their dog back down to the box area again for another round – do three or four rounds total. Everybody usually leaves the class worn out and laughing after this drill.

Dogs are ready to move up to the intermediate class if they can do the following things consistently:

- Run a full recall over four jumps

- Retrieve a ball (off the floor) and bring it back to their owner

- Complete a four-footed swimmer's turn on the box (without a ball)

- Work well around other dogs

Intermediate Class

Recalls

These never go out of style.

Box work

Introduce the ball if you haven't already done so, using a squishy foam ball or practice tennis ball if necessary. Add props strategically in front of and around the box to get the best approach and foot placement. Gradually increase distance and ramp up the motivators (dog's handler running away and calling him, another person running next to dog) to increase speed off the box.

Passing

Introduce the dogs to passing using the passing drills described earlier in the book.

Side-by-side racing

Once a dog is able to complete full runs to the box and back, add a dog into the other lane for him to race against. Use ring gating in between the lanes at first if necessary and gradually phase it out.

Some dogs will be practically ready for competition after a few months of intense classes. Others will not.

If a student from class has been bitten by the flyball bug and wants to compete, you need to decide with the rest of the club ahead of time how to want to approach it. You can invite them to join your club, let them race with your club on a trial basis, encourage them to race in the Open division (and support them by putting a few dogs from your club on that team), or refer them to other clubs in the area.

Remember that anybody you invite to join your club will be spending a lot of time with you. They'll be attending your practices regularly and attending tournaments with you. If you or anybody on your club has issues with somebody from flyball class, think long and hard about inviting them to join your club. Also, make sure that you discuss your club's goals with them ahead of time to prevent misunderstandings and conflicts later on.

What to Expect at a Flyball Tournament

We all train in hopes that one day our dog will be ready to play in the big leagues at a real flyball tournament.

Flyball tournaments are usually two full days of non-stop racing – they start around 8 a.m. and end late in the afternoon. Usually schedules are front-loaded with more races on Saturday than Sunday so that the tournament can wrap up mid-afternoon on Sunday. That way everybody can attend the awards ceremony and still get on the road at a reasonable time. Unless there's a lunch break (which you rarely see anymore), there will be a team warming up or racing in the ring every minute of the tournament. Expect to be sore on Monday morning!

Before the Tournament

To find out about upcoming tournaments in your area, consult NAFA's or U-FLI's website – they both have prominent links to tournament listings right on their home pages. If you subscribe to any of the regional Yahoo groups, you will also get tournament announcements and reminders that way.

Entries and paperwork

Most tournaments **close** (stop accepting entries) about a month before the tournament date. Almost every flyball club has a website these days, so you should be able to find all the information you need there – the closing date, which classes are offered (Regular, Multibreed/Variety, Open, Veterans, etc.), the entry form, a list of nearby hotels, and directions. Several days before the tournament, the host club will also post a Welcome Letter plus the final seed chart and racing schedule for you to download and print.

Tournament directors will almost always accept a tournament entry via email – it is actually common practice to send your entry via email (just include your club name, a list of your teams, what class of racing each team will be in, and their seed times) and put your hard-copy entry form and check in the mail on the same day.

You don't need to know which dogs will be running yet (although you might already know that); you just need to submit seed times for now.

It makes the tournament director's life a lot easier if you can send your entry fee in as one check from your club, versus lots of little individual checks from your teammates.

Racing numbers

Every dog needs a racing number before he can compete. Racing numbers are cheap and easy to get, and they're a one-time expenditure per dog. You don't need them when you send your tournament paperwork in – you need them when you fill out your actual time sheet for that team (usually that's Saturday morning 30 minutes before racing starts).

- **NAFA:** "Competition Racing Number" (CRN), costs $25. Purchase it on the NAFA website (http://www.flyball.org).

- **U-FLI:** "Race Utility Number" (RUN), costs $10. Purchase it on the U-FLI website (http://www.u-fli.com). U-FLI also requires that you create a "Participant Number" for yourself before registering any dogs (this is free).

Logistics

Make sure everybody in your club has directions to the tournament and knows where to find the Welcome Letter, list of hotels, directions, and schedule. Clubs usually work with the nearby dog-friendly hotels on group rates, so reserve your hotel room as early as you can, otherwise you might end up driving farther and paying high pet fees.

Finalize your lineups, including which dogs will be listed in the warm-up slots. Make a list of jobs for each team member on each team (i.e. who will handle the dogs, box load, help with warm-ups, shag balls, call passes, etc.).

It is really helpful if somebody in your club is willing to make a list of all your club's races, color code them by team, then laminate them into little cards that you can carry around in your pocket or clip to a lanyard. You don't need a fancy laminating machine; you can buy self-adhesive laminating sheets at Target, Wal-Mart or any office supply store.

Don't forget to bring all the dogs' racing numbers and a list of your teammates' cell phone numbers!

Practice and conditioning

Lay off heavy running and conditioning at least three days before a tournament. Some flyball competitors joke that they wrap their dogs in bubble wrap the whole week before a tournament.

If your team practices the night or two before a tournament, take it easy on the dogs who will be competing – just do some light box work or a lineup or two, and work more with your green dogs and puppies instead.

During the Tournament

Tournament site

Many competitors like to drop by the tournament site on Friday afternoon or evening to scope out the site and drop off their equipment (boxes, props, balls). The host club is usually setting up the ring at this time and will have the building open to competitors.

Sometimes host clubs will also offer single-dog racing on Friday nights, which is a great opportunity to get your green dog some ring time without a lot of pressure. U-FLI's singles and pairs racing is more formal (you usually have to register for it when you send in the original entry form), while single-dog racing at a NAFA tournament is more of a laid back practice-type of environment.

Although most tournaments start at 8 a.m. on Saturday, plan to get there an hour earlier, because you'll need time to get all your equipment into the building and fill out your lineup sheets to turn in at the score table. The judge inspects all the boxes prior to racing, and there's usually a "captains meeting" (although anybody can attend) where the tournament director goes over the racing format, warm-up times, and gives everybody the usual "Clean up after your dogs" speech. If you have a height dog that needs to be measured, that will also happen sometime before racing starts on Saturday (usually around 7:30 a.m.).

Clubs tend to cluster together all weekend long, either in the tournament building, the grassy areas surrounding the building, or in sections of the parking lot/RV areas. Crating areas can be simple or elaborate. Some clubs really go all out, setting up tents with exercise pens for the dogs, a ring of chairs for the humans, and a large table to hold the food spread.

Large scale crating area at the 2012 NAFA CanAm Classic. **(Photo by Dave Strauss)**

I prefer to crate out of my car if the weather is nice – that way I don't have to lug around a bunch of crates and my dogs stay relatively quiet and relaxed. I just park right next to our crating area, open up the side doors or the back of my van so the dogs get some air, and pull my chair out so I can sit with my teammates. I know it's probably not great for my car's engine, but if it's hot I'll leave the car running and the air conditioner on (with one window cracked, just in case the car decides to lock itself) so the dogs are comfortable.

Ring setup

If there are more than 40 teams entered into the tournament, it usually needs to be raced in two rings, meaning the host club is responsible for running two independent sets of racing lanes, lights, and judges.

🐕 *Typical two-ring setup.*

These days, clubs who host two-ring tournaments usually employ a "one schedule two-ring" format (versus two totally different schedules), meaning that whatever race is up next goes into the soonest available ring. This speeds things up a lot, but also requires clubs to be hyper-aware of what's going on in the racing lanes because that will determine what ring they're in next. It can get really confusing if your club has several teams entered and/or you also have a dog running in the Open or Veteran's division with people from another club.

There will be a race counter (either digital or the old flip-chart style) placed near the score table so competitors can keep track of what race is going on. Sometimes the host clubs will make the number on the race counter the *on deck* race (instead of which race is actually in the lanes) to give competitors an early heads up. Those sorts of details are covered in the captains meeting before racing begins.

The average pace of racing is about 7-8 races per hour for a one-ring tournament and 12-15 races per hour for a two-ring setup (slightly slower average per ring because of ring conflicts and delays). So if it's a one-ring tournament and you have an eight-race break, you have time to go get some lunch or take a nap (lucky you).

Wrapping your dog's feet

Some competitors like to wrap their dog's feet as a preventive measure. Not every dog needs to be wrapped, but there are some with soft pads whose feet get burned running on the mats all weekend long. I have a dog whose dew claw will get snagged on the box for some reason – she has ripped her dew claws off a few times this way (ouch!), so I now wrap her front legs to cover the dew claws and carpal pad areas.

Dragon the Whippet with four wrapped legs. **(Photo by Len Silvester)**

The Beginner's Guide to Flyball

If you have a dog that slides into the box on his way down the lane, you might also find that taping all four of his feet and/or legs will give him that extra bit of traction he needs to prevent the sliding.

If you wrap your dog as a preventive measure (versus waiting until his feet are sore), the wrap job can be very simple and quick. You don't need any padding or gauze under the wrap because you're just adding a layer of protection to healthy pads.

I use Andover's PowerFlex (although 3M's Vetwrap and Andover's Co-Flex are also good). I like PowerFlex because it has a high tensile strength, so it doesn't wear through or shred off. It also doesn't tighten up if it gets wet. (Plus it comes in camouflage print! Plus about 20 other colors.) You can buy it in bulk online or even through your veterinarian.

Wrap it around the dog's feet or carpal/dew claw area a few times – snug but not too tight, because you don't want to cut off the circulation. The great thing about all of these wraps is that you can tear them off the roll with your hands, and then simply grip them with your hand to seal them onto the dog's feet/legs. I don't even use tape to hold them on.

Cut the wraps off after every race and reapply them before the next race to give the dog's feet/legs a chance to breathe and to make sure the wrap doesn't roll up and chafe a sore spot on the bottom of their foot.

Racing

When you're the next team up to race, it's called being "on deck" (if you're two races out, you're "in the hole"). That's the time to take your dog out of his crate, walk him around to stretch out his muscles, and make sure he has a chance to potty. Make time for this before every race! The dogs are keyed up and drinking a lot of water, and if they foul in the ring you'll lose that heat automatically. Then make your way over to the ring (or wait right outside the door of the building if your dog gets too excited next to the ring) and wait for your turn to go in. Your warm-up time is limited, so you want to be ready to walk into the ring as soon as the other race is over.

During warm-ups make sure your team sets the jumps to the proper height and that somebody (usually the pass caller) tells the line judge which dogs are racing.

Setting jump heights before the race. *(Photo by Dave Strauss)*

When the warm-up time is over, the judge will blow the whistle and the teams will line up in the runback area to await the start of the race.

If the judge blows his whistle at any point during the actual race, hold your dog – a whistle usually indicates something serious enough to stop the race, like interference or a box malfunction.

After the race, thank the other team (by shaking hands, saying "Good race" or something along those lines) and exit the ring as quickly as possible so the next teams can come in and warm up.

Tournament jobs

I've listed out a lot of jobs below, but obviously the ones you can't live without are the four handlers and the box loader.

If you are in a small club or are going to be short-handed for a tournament, you can send out an email ahead of time to your region's email list and ask if anybody wants to trade help for help – usually you will get several takers.

Handler

A person who runs a dog during a race. If you're the handler of a green dog who's warming up but not racing in the actual race, you may get assigned one of the jobs below once warm-ups are over.

Handlers are responsible for getting their dogs into the ring on time, participating in warm-ups (if your dog needs one), and racing. If the team is really short-handed and the handler's dog isn't too hard to manage, the handler may also be called upon to help set jump heights during warm-ups or shag balls in the runback during racing.

Box loader

A person who loads balls into the box during the race. Responsibilities also include getting box and balls ready and setting up props for warm-ups.

This job can be a little tricky for newbies, especially if they're loading the box for a very fast team and/or the dogs on the team take all sorts of different types of balls in different holes.

It helps to have big pockets or wear an apron, since you'll need to have some extra balls on hand in case one or more of the dogs has to re-run.

Box loaders are not allowed to clap for dogs or point at the ball because it's considered to be training in the ring, but they *are* allowed to talk to them and call them. (Box loaders are also allowed to use subtle hand signals for deaf dogs). Box loaders can step off the box at any time during the race to get more balls, but as a courtesy to the other team they should not move off the box until the judge declares the race over (if the other team has already lost but is re-running dogs).

Pass caller

A person who stands behind the line judge at the start/finish line and tells the team how accurate their passes are.

Some pass callers watch the race and hold up fingers to indicate the size (in feet) of each pass as it's happening, while others videotape the race and play back the passes in slow motion as soon as the race is over. The second method is more accurate but also takes more time and technical know-how.

🐾 *Hawkeye Hustlers videotaping their passes during the 2011 U-FLI Tournament of Champions.* **(Photo by Len Silvester)**

The pass caller is usually the one to tell the team's lineup to the Line Judge. You don't need to tell them each dog's name – just look at the sheet and tell them which numbers to circle (dogs # 1, 2, 3 & 5, for example).

Statistician

A person who stands on the sidelines and writes down all the team's times that appear on the digital display – this includes start times, split times for each dog, and total time at the end of each heat.

Most clubs have some sort of template they like to use for stats, depending on what data they're tracking. Some statisticians also consult with the pass caller during or after the race and record what each pass was next to each split time. This passing information can be really helpful when it comes time to analyze each dog's performance – if a pass is very large, the dog's time is going to look a lot slower on the stats sheet than it actually was from line-to-line.

🐕 *This is six-year-old Peyton Perry of the Weston Whirlwinds flyball team. Peyton's mom, Renee, says Peyton has been exposed to flyball since birth and her nickname is the "puppy whisperer" because all dogs like her. In addition to ball shagging, Peyton is also helping train her mom's dogs and is running teammate Cindy Henderson's dogs.* **(Photo by Dave Strauss)**

Ball shagger

A person who stands in the runback area with the team and picks up loose balls before they become a safety hazard or interfere with the other team.

Most clubs use a metal tennis ball hopper to pick up balls during the race, and then return the balls to a large bucket or Tupperware container down by the box immediately following the race.

Other jobs

If the club is big enough, there will be people left over to help even after all the jobs are covered (what a luxury!). These people can help with warm-ups – it's great to have a lot of people hustling around setting up jumps, setting up props, holding dogs for recalls, clapping for dogs, running with dogs, etc. They can also videotape the race (box turns, passes, or the entire run), which provides the team with a lot of helpful feedback later on.

Line judge

A person who sits in the chair at the start/finish line and notifies the judge (by waving a flag) of any errors that would require a dog to re-run, such as an early pass, dropped ball, dog running around a jump, etc. There's a line judge for each lane.

The line judge is also responsible for recording which dogs are racing in each heat, whether the team in their lane won or lost, and what that team's final time was each heat.

Competitors are encouraged to line judge and box judge when they're not racing. Line judging is a little tricky for newbies, but it will only take a few minutes to learn if you ask an experienced person to explain it to you, and it's a great front-row seat to the action. Often there's a raffle just for line and box judges, too – every race you judge you get a ticket that goes into a raffle for money or a nice prize. A little extra incentive!

Box judge

A person who sits in the chair down by the box and notifies the judge (by waving a flag) of any errors that would require a dog to re-run. Common errors at the box include not triggering the box properly (dog is "stealing" the ball), dropping a ball, or running around a jump.

Raffle

Almost every club has some sort of raffle table at their tournament – it's a great way for them to earn extra money (and sometimes it's the only way they make a profit or break even). Usually the prizes are raffled off around 2 p.m. on Sunday.

After the Tournament

As soon as the last race of the tournament is over, people will start scrambling like mad to clean up and take all their equipment out to the car while the judge, score table, and tournament director tally up the points and determine the placements for each division of racing.

The Beginner's Guide to Flyball

When the results are finalized (usually 20-30 minutes after the last race), all the clubs gather for the awards ceremony. Sometimes other awards are given out in addition to the tournament placements, such as new titles, unique awards (like the "Perfect Start" award for a handler who gets a .000 start), and plaques/certificates for big accomplishments from NAFA or U-FLI. Award ceremonies are informal, celebratory and fun.

Tournament results (including point totals for each dog) are entered into the NAFA or U-FLI databases and become part of the permanent record.

General Tournament Etiquette

Here are some things to keep in mind while at a flyball tournament:

- Remember that everybody yells during flyball – most of the time people aren't trying to be mean, they're just trying to be heard over the barking dogs.

- This is really a no-brainer, but clean up after your dogs at all times.

- Don't distract the racing dogs when you're watching from the sidelines. Bringing a lunging, barking dog or a squeaky toy or food right next to the lane can wreak havoc on a racing dog's focus. Also, don't be offended if someone asks you to back up away from their dog or the sidelines, because some dogs are really sensitive.

- If you're crating inside, there's nothing more annoying than having a dog near your crating area going ballistic in his crate and barking all day. If your dog does this, leave him in the car, or outside, or put a sheet over his crate (if this actually works).

- Box loaders: Don't step off the box during the race unless it's to get more balls. It's considered poor sportsmanship if your team has finished racing but the other team hasn't and you're off the box putting away your equipment or whatever.

- If your dog bobbles into the other lane or crosses over to chase another dog, move quickly to get your dog under control. It really upsets people when a dog crosses over (this includes the runback area, too, not just the racing lanes), so take quick action, and then apologize to the other team.

- If you have a female dog that is in heat, leave her at home. She's not allowed to race and her presence there will distract other dogs.

- If your dog pees in the community kiddie pool (happens all the time!) dump the pool out and refill it with clean water.

Tournament Checklist

Here are some common things people bring to flyball tournaments:

- Extra socks and shoes (in case it rains or your feet get wet walking through wet grass in the early morning).

- Extra clothes for Saturday – if you leave all your spare clothes in your hotel room, you will inevitably get bled on, peed on, or your shirt will get ripped.

- A chair.

- A cooler with drinks and snacks in it.

- Water from home (or bottled water) for you dog(s). Some dogs have sensitive tummies and get diarrhea if they drink tap water from somewhere else.

- Extra collapsible crates or exercise pens. These are great if you don't want to unpack crates out of your car and carry them to the crating area and/or hotel room each day. Make sure your dog will actually stay in a soft crate or ex-pen at a loud, exciting tournament site, though – my dogs can only be trusted in them in the hotel room.

- Some sort of sheet or cover for the top of your dog's crate (especially if you have a barker).

- Foot/leg wrap (and tape, scissors, and gauze if your wrap routine is more complicated) for dogs that need to be wrapped.

- Some sort of pain reliever medicine (for you). I usually take several ibuprofen on Sunday morning!

- Treats for the dogs during the day, to help them keep their energy up. A little peanut butter or other protein works great.

You're Addicted – Now What?

Most of us discover flyball after we already have a dog – we're looking for a fun game to play with our dog, or we enjoy hanging out with other dog people, or our dog has a lot of energy and needs a "job," so voila! We start playing flyball.

Then we get hooked. And we get competitive.

Adding Another Dog

For some people, getting more competitive means getting another dog. Maybe the dog you are playing flyball with now is a getting older or he prefers being a couch potato to a more athletic lifestyle. Perhaps you've fallen in love with a new breed or type of dog after spending time with them in the flyball lanes – that's how I ended up getting my first Border Collie after years of owning only Jack Russell Terriers.

Maybe you want a faster dog, or a smaller dog (if your team desperately needs height dogs, for instance), or a more biddable type of dog (although there's no guarantee with this one…I've had Border Collies who took longer to train than terriers!). Maybe you've really improved as a trainer and want to train a young dog from scratch, in hopes that this time you'll train a beautiful box turn or a turbo recall from the beginning.

Whatever the reason, getting a new dog is a big, exciting decision.

So what should you get?

If you have a specific breed in mind, this one is a no-brainer, but if you just know you want a "faster" dog, or if you only have experience with big dogs and know you want a "height dog," here are some things to keep in mind.

Breed

A quick analysis of NAFA's breed database reveals that these are the top ten flyball breeds in order of popularity:

❶ Border Collie

❷ Mixed breed

❸ Australian Shepherd (Aussie)

❹ Jack Russell Terrier

❺ Labrador Retriever

❻ Shetland Sheepdog (Sheltie)

❼ Golden Retriever

❽ Australian Cattle Dog

❾ Cocker Spaniel

❿ Doberman Pinscher

Although they still make the NAFA top 10, there aren't as many Dobermans, German Shepherds, or Cocker Spaniels playing flyball these days. NAFA has been keeping records for 25 years and has over 100,000 dogs registered in its database, so I believe these rankings still reflect the earlier years of flyball, where you were more likely to see breeds used in competitive obedience (because these were the same trainers first getting involved in flyball).

You'll still see a ton of Border Collies, Shelties, Jack Russells, Golden Retrievers and Labrador Retrievers in the lanes – if you're looking for a purebred flyball prospect, it's hard to go wrong with one of these breeds (as long as you're prepared for all the energy that comes with them). Many mixed breeds excel in flyball as well.

Newer flyball trends include Whippets, Staffordshire Bull Terriers, Belgian Shepherds (Malinois and Tervurens), and intentionally-bred mixes.

In the past ten years or so, the intentionally-bred mixes (sometimes referred to in the dog world as "designer dogs") have become very popular and common in flyball. It started out with experimental breedings to create a faster type of height dog – people crossed Border Collies and Jack Russell Terriers ("Border Jacks") and Border Collies and Border Terriers ("Border Borders"). From there it evolved to Border Collies and Staffordshire Bull Terriers ("Border Staffies"), Border Collie and Whippets ("Border Whippets"), and even mixes to mixes (Border Jacks to Border Staffies, for example).

Punk and Seek are seven-year-old Border Staffies from the same litter. *(Photo by Stephanie Minnella)*

These mixes have proven, in many cases, to be stronger, faster, and often healthier than the purebreds. The first team to break into the 15's was Rocket Relay with a Border Border height dog back in the early 2000s. Spring Loaded set their NAFA world records with a Border Staffy height dog, and Touch N Go's 2011 U-FLI world record was set with two Border Staffies and two Border Whippets.

The formation of U-FLI has further ratcheted up the demand for these intentional mixes, because dogs that would be too big to run as a NAFA height dog can play the role of U-FLI height dog (due to the way U-FLI measures) and still run just as fast or faster than the "big dogs" on the team.

The intentional mixes are thoughtfully bred – most of the breeders of these dogs are diligent about getting health checks done on the parents and breeding the best to the best in terms of structure, drive, and temperament. As a result the designer mixes are highly sought after. Some people have compared getting on the list for one of these pups to finding a Golden Ticket in a Willie Wonka chocolate bar.

Height

If you're hoping for a (NAFA) height dog, you'll need one who doesn't grow any taller than 17 inches at the withers (earlier in the book I talked about how 11 inches seems to be the limit that most dogs can jump and still maintain their speed).

When NAFA lowered its jump height by an inch in 2008 (from four inches to five inches below the withers), it made it easier for the slightly bigger "borderline" dogs to jump their own jump height. This meant a lot of the larger Shelties, Staffordshire Bull Terriers, and mixes could suddenly be considered as height dog prospects.

Jack Russells make fantastic height dogs because they are very quick and strong. They can run all weekend long over their own jump height like little machines. A few years ago, most Division 1 teams were made up of three Border Collies and a Jack Russell Terrier height dog, but these days more and more mixes are taking over the role of height dog. The risk with getting a mix as your height dog prospect is that there's no guarantee that he'll actually end up under 17 inches tall, whereas you can pretty much guarantee that a Jack Russell or other small purebred will stay at or below 15 inches.

Qualities to look for

Look for a puppy or adult dog with a great temperament and a lot of drive, because it will make your life sooooo much easier. Don't get sucked in by looks! Make sure whatever dog you pick is interested in playing with you and carries himself in a confident, pleasant manner.

🐕 *Laura Moretz's five-week-old litter of Border Staffies socializing with my son, Connor. We ended up picking the pup on the ground by Connor's face, but they were all wonderful.* **(Photo by Laura Moretz)**

Bring a ball and a tug with you when you evaluate the dog, and see if he will chase a ball or tug with you. You really want a puppy that wants to interact with you – this will make for a great foundation in any sport including flyball.

If you're trying to pick between several puppies, watch how each pup acts toward the others – don't pick the bully.

It often helps to speak with the breeder about your training strengths and weaknesses, plus your lifestyle and home situation. The breeders have evaluated the puppies since they were born and have a good idea for what type of home would be ideal for each puppy's personality.

You should also choose a dog with a well-balanced, athletic body. Poor structure will get in the way of a dog's flyball performance – straight shoulders or a straight rear make it hard for them to run or jump efficiently.

If you want to learn more about dog structure, look for a Pat Hastings seminar in your area (her website is http://www.dogfolk.com), or read the book *Dogsteps* by Rachel Page Elliot.

You're Addicted – Now What?

Also, try to evaluate as many litters of puppies as you can, even if you're not ready to get one yet or it's not a breed or breeding you would be interested in. This way you can compare the litter you are eventually interested in to the other litters – it's nice to have that basis of comparison.

Where should you get the dog?

Breeders

If you have something specific in mind – you want a purebred with registration papers, for example, or one of the intentionally-bred mixes – you will want to find a reputable breeder.

There's a big difference between a dog bred for performance and a dog bred to be a pet (and/or for conformation shows). Performance dogs are usually built differently (lighter boned, more angulation) and have more drive, meaning they would much rather be out chasing something or working versus sitting on the couch.

Good breeders spend a lot of time evaluating their dogs and breeding them with specific characteristics in mind – performance breeders produce light, agile, high-drive dogs that excel in dog sports or working (herding, hunting), while conformation/show or pet breeders tend to produce more laid back dogs that align with the breed standard.

Here are a few ways to find good performance dog breeders:

- **Tournaments.** If you see a dog at a tournament that you really like, approach the owner and ask where they got him (obviously use common sense and don't ask them when they're walking into the racing lane). Most people will be happy to chat about their dog with his admirers.

- **Facebook.** There are a bunch of flyball competitors on Facebook. Start networking! Don't be obnoxious about it, but also don't be shy – I am "friends" with lots of flyball people on Facebook who I have actually never met or even spoken to, we just happen to share mutual contacts and interests. It won't be long before you are learning about who is getting puppies and where they are getting them (and oftentimes the breeders themselves are also on Facebook).

- **Google.** Most dog breeders these days have a website. Google the breed you're interested in plus the word "flyball" (or "agility") – that way you'll find people who are specifically breeding performance dogs (breeders like to tout their breeding program's accomplishments and titles, so words like "flyball" will come up in a search). You could also do very well with a dog from working lines, even if they haven't been bred with dog sports in mind – Jack Russell Terriers bred for hunting, Border Collies bred for herding, and Labradors bred for field trials will often possess the kind of structure and drive you're looking for in a flyball dog.

If you can't get on the puppy list that you want, or you can't afford to be on it (many performance pups are over $1,000 these days), don't despair. Many great flyball dogs come from humble beginnings (rescues, farm dogs, pet breeders) and there's no guarantee that the $1,200 Border Collie pup from a performance breeder will grow up to run sub-4 seconds.

Since you're getting this dog specifically to play flyball, you may want to get a puppy versus an adult dog. Most puppies are really open to new experiences and easier to socialize because they haven't reached that "fear period" stage of development yet (which often sets in around at five or six months), so you can expose them to all sorts of things – noisy tournaments, traveling in the car, other dogs, and loud noises like the "Bang!" of a flyball box triggering – and they'll roll with it. You can also teach them to be crazy little tuggers and ball retrievers, the earlier the better.

The other benefit to getting a puppy is that you'll get them before they develop any bad habits or fears. You're starting with a clean slate, essentially.

Rescues

Another option is to adopt a dog that has been rescued (a **rescue** is a dog who has been abandoned or given up by his owner to a rescue organization or an animal shelter. It's not really considered a "rescue" if a breeder decides, for instance, that she doesn't like the way a pup's ears are turning out so finds it a new home versus keeping it in her breeding program – that's a "rehoming").

Many rescue dogs make *great* flyball dogs. So often these dogs have been given up by their previous owners because they have "too much energy." This is a classic case of a dog needing a job or activity as an outlet for their energy, and once you get them into a performance home and start training them and putting them to work, they become ideal companions.

Some good places to look for a rescue dog are the local animal shelter, Petfinder (http://www.petfinder.com), various breed rescue organizations (such as Border Collie Rescue or Jack Russell Rescue), pet adoption events, plus Facebook and the various flyball email lists and Yahoo groups – people are always posting about available dogs here.

Your lifestyle

Carefully consider your household situation when deciding on your next dog. A rescue might not be for you, for instance, if you have several dogs already and a complicated pack dynamic. A few years ago I had two adult females who did not get along and had to be carefully managed, so adding another adult female into the mix would have just been asking for trouble. Instead, I chose a pup that grew up knowing her place in the pack order. I also have two young children, so any rescue I took in would have to be bombproof with kids – it's easier to train a young pup not to herd or nip children than an adult dog.

If you work away from home all day, on the other hand, you may be better off with an adult dog – it's nice to be able to bypass the housebreaking and teething stages and have a dog who doesn't have to be constantly monitored in the house (not a guarantee with an adult rescue, but many adults have already been housebroken and taught some basic obedience).

Also, an adult dog can be ready to compete as soon as you can get him trained, whereas a puppy can't play flyball until he turns one year old. So if you really need a height dog or are anxious to get another dog up and running as soon as possible, an adult dog (or older puppy) would be a good option.

Switching Clubs

Once you've been playing flyball for a year or so, you may realize that you'd be happier playing as part of a different club. This could happen for a number of reasons, the most common ones being:

- **Your philosophy is different from your club's.** Maybe they focus too much on their fast "A" team while you'd prefer to run for points, or you're the one that's become competitive while the rest of them could care less how fast they are as long as they're consistently earning points. Or they want to travel to everything within an eight-hour radius and you just want to play locally.

- **Personality differences.** Sometimes people just don't click. It's not much fun spending lots of time with people you don't get along with, especially if you have regular practices, frequent tournament weekends, or dinners out with the team.

- **Location.** If a new club starts up in your area (or you find some local flyball enthusiasts and start one yourself), it's a good reason to switch clubs, especially if you've been driving a long distance to and from practices.

- **You outgrow your team.** Sometimes you really want to improve and take it to the next level, but your club can't help you get there, so you look for a more experienced team who can take you under their wing and teach you a lot.

I've been in a lot of flyball clubs over the years and have switched clubs for all of the above reasons. My general feeling about it is this – I play flyball for fun. It is my hobby and I'm supposed to be having a good time doing it. If it's not fun, then what's the point?

Leaving a flyball club is sort of a cross between leaving a job and breaking up with a boyfriend/girlfriend. If you give the club enough notice (so that you're not leaving them hanging for a tournament you've already committed to, for example) and you're rational and calm as you explain why you're switching clubs, it usually goes pretty well. Some people may get upset with you because they feel rejected by you, or because the club really needs your dogs (especially if you're a height dog owner), but that's sort of how it goes when you switch jobs, too. You can't make everybody happy. The most important thing is that *you're* happy. If you can be happy without burning bridges, more power to you.

Try to leave on the best terms possible, though, because you are probably going to see your former club at every tournament you attend for many years to come. There's enough drama in flyball already. If you can salvage the relationship, you may even be able to help each other out at tournaments (box load or shag balls for each other, for example), run together from time to time on an Open/Pickup team, or even practice together.

Wait period

NAFA and U-FLI both have wait periods to discourage club hopping (the rules were mainly put into place so that people wouldn't put together "dream teams" of fast dogs for one weekend, then go right back to running with their regular club the next weekend). NAFA's wait period is 87 days and U-FLI's is 120 days. In the old days, you really had to sit your dog out that long – it was quite a deterrent to switching clubs. (NAFA and U-FLI only keep track of the dogs, not the people. *You* can play with any club you want at any time, it's just your dog that has to stick with one or the other.)

These days you can play Open/Pickup or Veterans during the wait period, so it's not nearly as painful. If your new club really wants you to run with them and they don't care about regional points (which count towards regional championships if you race in Division 1), they can just enter their teams with your dogs as Open/Pickup or Veterans teams for a few tournaments until the wait period is over. Or you can create an Open/Pickup or Veterans team with friends or acquaintances from a few other clubs and just race for fun in the meantime, and still be at the tournament to help your new club out.

There is nothing "official" you need to do, from a NAFA or U-FLI perspective, to switch clubs. Nobody needs to be notified, no paperwork needs to be filled out. When you race your dog with your new club (after the wait period is over), your dog's points will be automatically recorded and assigned to the new club, and your dog's name will be transferred in the organizations' databases.

Taking it to the Next Level

After you've got the basics figured out, you may decide that flyball is something you want to get really good at. That happens to a lot of us. You start out playing for fun and get totally caught up in it.

So how do you get better/faster?

- **Attend a seminar.** You may need to travel, but it's worth it. Here are some highly accomplished clubs that put on exciting, professional seminars: Rocket Relay (Aaron Robbins and Kelly Robbins-Walt) from Ontario, X Flyball and Lickety Splits from San Diego, Slammers and Spring Loaded from Michigan, and Top Dog Racers from Texas.

- **Practice with another club.** Or switch clubs altogether. It's quite common for people from different clubs to practice together occasionally – either as a one-off thing (one person attends another club's practice to learn from someone more experienced) or as a group "scrimmage" sort of thing. Some clubs even share the same practice building or field on a regular basis.

- **Watch Division 1 races at tournaments.** You can learn a lot from just sitting on the sidelines and watching how the Division 1 teams do things – their warm-ups are like two-minute training sessions, and their races offer you a front-row view into how they operate (how they line up, call their dogs, get their dogs revved-up, call passes, or play with their dogs after each heat).

- **Videotape your dogs (during practices, tournaments, and at home training sessions).** You will learn so much just from watching your dogs on slow-motion playback.

- **Research flyball training information online.** These days you can find so much videotape and training information on Google, YouTube and Facebook. Get involved with the flyball community and absorb as much as you can.

- **Find a mentor.** Many people become friendly with a good trainer (possibly meeting them at a tournament or chatting with them via Facebook or email) and schedule time to hang out with them for private coaching (could include private lessons or just hanging out with their club at a tournament or practice).

Also, the only way you actually *know* you're getting better is if you keep track of your dog's times and your passes from tournament to tournament. Remember that your pass is included in your dog's total time (except start dogs in NAFA tournaments – their start time is split out from their line to line time), so to truly monitor your dog's progress you need to be videotaping the start/finish line so you can figure out your dog's line to line time. So many times I've thought my dogs were having a "bad weekend" when really my passes just sucked.

A Few Final Thoughts

Every time I work with a new dog I feel like a newbie all over again. Each dog has a unique learning style and is motivated by different things.

The best pieces of advice I can offer you when it comes to training and competing for flyball are:

- Remember that there are usually ten different ways to train each skill in flyball, so if something doesn't work with your dog, try a different method.

- Don't get caught up in analysis paralysis. Have you ever heard that saying "the perfect is the enemy of the good"? Don't worry about making your dog perfect – just do your best, learn from your mistakes, and enjoy the time you spend with your dog and your teammates.

- Be a good sport and take the time to smile and chat with other competitors – flyball is a small, tight-knit community and you'll be seeing all these people at tournaments, hopefully for years to come. You may even meet some of your best friends this way.

- Stay positive and have fun, because flyball is just a game and all your dog really wants to do is to play with you.

Good luck with your training – I hope to see you in the lanes someday!

Please stop by my website at http://www.flyballpropaganda.com for ongoing discussions and the master Resources list (there is one at the end of this book, but the one on my website will always be more up-to-date and more comprehensive). And feel free to reach out to me at xterrier@gmail.com with any questions or comments.

Resources

A more comprehensive list with up-to-the-minute URLs can be found on my website: **http://www.flyballpropaganda.com** (click on the "Flyball Resources" tab).

General

North American Flyball Association (http://www.flyball.org) NAFA is the largest governing body in flyball.

United Flyball League International (http://www.u-fli.com) U-FLI is the newer governing body.

Flyball Home Page (http://www.flyballdogs.com) This site has been around forever and is pretty outdated (in terms of general info, equipment, etc.) but still hosts a lot of the flyball teams' websites on it, so it's a good place to start if you're looking for a team in your area.

Karen Pryor Clicker training (http://www.clickertraining.com) Karen was one of the early pioneers of teaching clicker training to dogs.

Len Silvester's photography (http://www.ttlphoto.com) Len is one of my favorite people I've never met (we have been online friends since 2006). He has always been a huge supporter of the flyball community, providing free photos for the NAFA website & marketing brochure, flyball articles in DogSport magazine, and this book. His action photos are stunning, whether it's a dog captured in spit-trail glory on a flyball box or a snowy owl in flight in the Minesing Wetlands of Ontario, Canada. Check out his website and you'll see what I mean.

Dave Strauss's photography (http://dwstrauss.smugmug.com) I stumbled onto Dave's photos about a month before I published this book – talk about a treasure trove! And he was kind enough to let me use anything I wanted. His photos are exceptional.

William Moore's photography (http://www.wmconsulting.com) Willie lives in Alabama and photographs (and competes in) a lot of flyball tournaments in the Southeastern U.S. Like Len, he's generously given me many photos over the years for the NAFA website, DogSport magazine, and this book. Click on "Flyball Pictures" in the left navigation. (Every tournament album has its own "Candids" folder – these are my favorite. Willie has a gift for capturing the spirit and camaraderie of flyball in and out of the ring.)

Flyball Today (http://www.livestream.com/flyballtoday) Provides livestream flyball most weekends.

Flyball Boxes

Premier flyball box (http://www.premierflyballbox.com) These high-quality plastic boxes are made by Dan Phillips in Michigan.

Synergy flyball box (http://www.synergyflyball.com/contact.htm) Designed by Kevin Hesse.

Miller flyball box (http://www.millerflyball.com) Designed by Mike Miller.

Tindall flyball box (eric@u-fli.com) Designed by Eric Tindall in Michigan.

Freda flyball box (http://www.flyballequip.com/flyballboxes.htm) Designed by Mike Freda.

Fast Track flyball box (http://www.fasttrackflyballbox.com) Designed by David Dubois.

Willoughby Workshop's box plans (with parts) (http://www.flyballequip.com/plans.htm) Includes plans and parts for 2-hole flyball box.

Other Flyball Equipment

Willoughby Workshop's FREE equipment plans (http://www.flyballequip.com/flyballjumps.html) Includes plans for 2-hole flyball box, plywood flyball jumps, props, and ring gating anchors).

Paul Ferlitto's Sintra flyball jumps and props (runndogs@gmail.com)
Paul is located in Alabama.

Crash Test toys (http://www.pathcom.com/~crasher) Great flyball tugs (my Border Staffy Punk loves his real fur tug made from a recycled fur coat…and the bungee handle it's attached to saves my arm).

"Skid boots"(http://webpages.charter.net/dhfm/ZControl.html) Reusable foot wraps made by Kathleen Hansen.

Foam balls at Oriental Trading Company (http://www.orientaltrading.com) Search on "foam ball" (there are different sizes).

Tuff-Spun mats (http://www.crown-mats.com/products/tuffspunrolls.html) Crown Mats (choose 3/8-inch mat, usually in 3-foot x 60-foot rolls).

Email Lists and Groups

NAFA News Yahoo group (http://pets.groups.yahoo.com/group/NAFANews) Announcements from the North American Flyball Association.

U-FLI Announcements Google group (http://groups.google.com/group/ufli) Announcements from U-FLI.

NAFA's Flyball Locator (http://www.flyball.org/getstarted) Lists regional email groups and websites by state/province.

The Flyball email list (http://www.flyballdogs.com/email-list.html) This list has been around since 1995 and has thousands of members. It is rarely used nowadays but it's still good to know about.

Blogs

Flyball Prop-a-Ganda (http://www.flyballpropaganda.com) My blog.

The Flyball Blog (http://www.flyballblog.com) This blog, run by Larry Worrilow, has been around since 2007 and contains a lot of great posts about training and flyball politics.

Susan Garrett's blog (http://www.susangarrettdogagility.com) Although Susan writes primarily about agility, she has some great posts about building killer recalls on dogs and other general performance-related content.

Suggested Reading

***DogSport* magazine (http://www.dogsportmagazine.com)** Regular coverage of flyball, mixed in with articles about agility, disc dog, obedience, dock diving, weight pull, and feature articles about training dogs for all levels of competition.

***The Culture Clash* by Jean Donaldson** There is so much great information you can pull from this book to help you with flyball training – how to build a great recall, how to become the ultimate reward to your dog, plus exercises for getting tentative tuggers to tug and reluctant ball retrievers to retrieve. All presented with a very positive training style, backed up by behavioral science. Plus, Donaldson is really funny.

***Dogsteps: A New Look* by Rachel Page Elliot** A fantastic book about dog structure and movement. Elliott teaches us about dogs' gait and how it relates to physical activities such as flyball, and she includes many sketches and diagrams, all based on actual "moving x-rays" of dogs running on a treadmill from Harvard's zoology lab.

***Ruff Love* by Susan Garrett** One of the first dog training books I ever read. Garrett's focus is on building a great relationship between you and your dog *before* you let him have full run of the house or play with your other dogs. Her book teaches you how to create a great work ethic in your dog, which makes it especially good for people with new puppies or easily-distracted adult dogs.

***When Pigs Fly! Training Success With Impossible Dogs* by Jane Killion** I loved this book because I've always had at least three Jack Russell Terriers running around my house, and Killion's quirky Bull Terriers remind me of them. Killion teaches you how to work with "impossible dogs" by leveraging their natural behaviors to achieve success in the performance world. Her methods really work, and she includes lots of photos to illustrate her points. Distracted, unmotivated pets can be transformed into focused flyball machines with the right training – this book will help you get there.

***Control Unleashed* by Leslie McDevitt** This book has been enthusiastically embraced by the agility community, and has a lot to offer owners of flyball dogs as well. McDevitt's methods help build focus and confidence in dogs that have difficulty concentrating or working off lead in a stimulating environment (which is pretty much what any flyball class, practice or tournament is). My club used several of the exercises in this book to get my Border Collie Kraken (the herder) ready to compete.

The Power of Positive Dog Training **by Pat Miller** Miller explains clicker training in layman's terms and walks you through, step-by-step, how to train a variety of basic commands using her positive methods and principles. A superb foundational book for flyball training.

Don't Shoot the Dog **by Karen Pryor** Any of Karen's books about clicker training are great. Learning how to clicker train your dog will give you a huge advantage in your flyball training – you will find your dog progressing through all the foundational work at light speed.

Peak Performance: Coaching the Canine Athlete **and** *Jumping from A to Z* **by Christine Zink** These are the kinds of books you'll find yourself poring over when you've shifted from the "pet dog" mindset to the "canine athlete" mindset. Zink is a veterinarian and an authority on dogs as athletes, and her books educate dog sport competitors on conditioning, feeding, structure, and performance-related injuries.

Seminars

Pat Hastings' *Puppy Puzzle* **seminar (http://www.dogfolk.com)** I've been to three of these and learned something new every time about dog structure and how it relates to flyball performance.

Rocket Relay flyball seminars (http://www.rocketrelay.net/seminars. html) Aaron Robbins and Kelly Robbins-Walt from Rocket Relay flyball team in Ontario (NAFA World Record holders at press time) travel all over the world putting on seminars. I've been to three over the last ten years and have come away with great new training ideas and insight every time.

Slammers flyball seminars (http://www.flyballdogs.com/slammers) Put on by Craig Knowles and Kristie Schultz from the Slammers flyball team in Michigan.

Spring Loaded flyball seminars (http://www.springloadedflyball.com)
Put on by Lee and Angie Heighton from Spring Loaded flyball team in Michigan (NAFA Multibreed World Record holders).

Top Dog Racers (http://www.topdogdallas.com/Flyball.htm) Put on by the Top Dog Racers flyball team in Texas.

About the Author

Lisa Pignetti has been playing flyball since 2000 and is currently training with X Flyball and Lickety Splits in San Diego, CA. She has five dogs that are either competing in flyball or training for flyball.

She served on the North American Flyball Association (NAFA) Board of Directors for two years (2007 and 2008) and was head of the marketing committee during this time. She was also NAFA's webmaster from 2005-2008. She has played both NAFA and U-FLI flyball all over North America.

Lisa and her Border Collie Sky also performed as part of the flyball act in **DOGS: The Incredible Show** in 2011.

Lisa has written several articles for *DogSport* magazine about various aspects of flyball training and writes a blog about flyball called Flyball Prop-a-Ganda (http://www.flyballpropaganda.com).

You can reach her at xterrier@gmail.com.

Printed in Great Britain
by Amazon